MILI PSYCHOLOGY

Volume 14, Number 2, 2002

Special Issue:
Chemical Warfare and Chemical Terrorism:
Psychological and Performance Outcomes
Guest Editors:
James A. Romano, Jr. and James M. King

*These articles were accepted under the editorship of Martin F. Wiskoff.

MILITARY PSYCHOLOGY, 2002, *14*(2), 83–84

Preface to the Special Issue

This special issue of *Military Psychology* reports behavioral, pharmacological, and toxicological science research on military performance as it is affected by chemical warfare agents (CWAs) and their pharmacological countermeasures. The five articles in this special issue were produced to complement the special issue of *Military Psychology* entitled "Effects of Chemical Protective Clothing on Military Performance" edited by Gerald P. Krueger and Louis E. Banderet in 1997. The articles in this issue are a diverse assembly: Some are very pharmacological in orientation, whereas others are driven by behavioral neuroscience. The unifying theme is the psychological consequences or organic syndromes that may be confused with psychological consequences resulting from exposure to CWAs or use of their medical countermeasures.

The principal classes of CWAs are nerve, blister, blood, and choking. The military CWA nomenclature adopted over 50 years ago emphasizes the principal target organ of each class of agent—central nervous system (CNS), skin or other epithelial tissue, blood and its oxygen-carrying capability, and the pulmonary system. CWAs were designed to be rapidly lethal (nerve, blood) or incapacitating (blister, choking) at relatively low concentrations. G nerve agents include tabun (GA), sarin (GB), soman (GD), and cyclosarin (GF). VX is another prominent nerve agent with versions used as weapons by both Cold War superpowers. The most prominent example of a blister agent is sulfur mustard (HD), but other significant examples include Lewisite (L) and phosgene oxime (CG). Of course, the most well-known and widely employed and studied blood and choking agents are cyanide and phosgene, respectively. These chemicals have long been considered traditional CWAs but may also be described as toxic industrial chemicals (TICs), which are toxic chemicals that reach a critical threshold of production that allows for their ready acquisition worldwide.

Both the threat of use and the actual use of CWAs will have important psychological and physiological consequences: The threat of CWA use can produce significant stress effects in affected populations; if CWAs are used, the psychological

This article is part of a special issue, "Chemical Warfare and Chemical Terrorism: Psychological and Performance Outcomes," of *Military Psychology,* 2002, *14*(2), 83–177.

Requests for reprints should be sent to Col. James A. Romano, Jr., U.S. Army Medical Research Institute of Chemical Defense, 3100 Rickerts Point Road, Aberdeen Proving Ground, MD 21010–5400.

impacts of both CNS and peripheral effects of the CWAs and their medical countermeasures must be considered. In the case of true exposures to nerve agents, chronic neurological sequelae can be expected in some cases, as can long-term posttraumatic stress disorder-like effects. Threatened or actual use of CWAs will require substantial mental health support to health care personnel and to the patient populations they support and will have major impacts on the health care system.

The guest editors of this special issue are James A. Romano, Jr., and James M. King. Col. Romano, who holds a doctorate in experimental psychology, currently serves as Commander of the U.S. Army Medical Research Institute of Chemical Defense at Aberdeen Proving Ground, Maryland, the Defense Department's premier laboratory for medical chemical defense research. Dr. King, who holds a doctorate in psychology from the University of Texas at Arlington, is Deputy Director of the Chemical and Biological Defense Information Analysis Center, which serves as the Department of Defense's focal point for information related to chemical and biological defense technology. For more information about either organization, visit their Web sites at http://usamricd.apgea.army.mil and http://www.cbiac.apgea.army.mil/

ACKNOWLEDGMENTS

This special issue reflects the integrated efforts of Department of Defense military and civilian scientists, technicians, and support personnel, along with their partners in academia and industry, who make up the Medical Chemical Defense Research Program.

James A. Romano, Jr.
James M. King
Guest Editors

MILITARY PSYCHOLOGY, 2002, *14*(2), 85–92

Chemical Warfare and Chemical Terrorism: Psychological and Performance Outcomes

James A. Romano, Jr.
Commander
U.S. Army Medical Research Institute of Chemical Defense
Aberdeen Proving Ground, Maryland

James M. King
Deputy Director
Chemical and Biological Defense Information Analysis Center
Aberdeen Proving Ground, Maryland

The battlefields of the late 20th century have come to include a significant new health threat: the use of modern chemical weapons. The potential to cause large numbers of serious casualties among deployed and deploying military forces and among civilian populations provides a stark reminder to medical planners of the limits of military and civilian medicine. However, medical countermeasures to these chemical warfare agents (CWAs) have been, and continue to be, developed. These CWAs, their countermeasures, and their health care implications are described in the articles of this special issue. These articles suggest likely psychological, physiological, and neurological effects that will be encountered should these agents be employed against U.S. forces on the integrated battlefield or against homeland facilities. Also suggested are countermeasures that U.S. forces and medical teams may use to protect or treat our forces or citizens undergoing such CWA attacks. Knowledge of the behavioral effects of the CWAs and of their medical countermeasures is imperative to ensure that military and civilian medical and mental health organizations can deal with possible incidents involving weapons of mass destruction. This first study, in contrast to the remaining studies in this special issue, focuses on the psychological factors in chemical warfare and terrorism. It also serves as an overview of the remaining articles in this special issue.

This article is part of a special issue, "Chemical Warfare and Chemical Terrorism: Psychological and Performance Outcomes," of *Military Psychology*, 2002, *14*(2), 83–177.

Requests for reprints should be sent to Col. James A. Romano, Jr., U.S. Army Medical Research Institute of Chemical Defense, 3100 Ricketts Point Road, Aberdeen Proving Ground, MD 21010–5400.

The integrated battlefield of the late 20th century has come to include a significant new health threat: modern chemical weapons. Traditionally, U.S. armed forces have been concerned with four classes of chemical warfare agents (CWAs): (a) choking (e.g., phosgene [CG]), (b) blood (e.g., cyanide [CN]), (c) blister (e.g., sulfur mustard [HD]), and (d) nerve agents (e.g., sarin [GB]). These agents differ in terms of rapidity of action, lethality, and the requirement for prompt or sustained medical care. Table 1 provides a summary of the major CWAs of concern, including their historical mortality/morbidity, principal target tissue, and proposed countermeasures. Their potential to cause large numbers of serious casualties provides a stark reminder to medical planners of the limits of military and civilian medicine. The articles in this issue suggest likely psychological, physiological, or neurological effects that will be encountered should these agents be used on the integrated battlefield or against homeland facilities and personnel. This latter eventuality is clearly an emerging threat, both to our military (Chandler & Backschies, 1998; Chandler & Trees, 1996) and civilian

TABLE 1
Twentieth-Century Morbidity of Four Classes of Chemical Warfare Agents and Their Principal Targets and Medical Countermeasures

Class of Chemical Warfare Agents	*Historic Lethality and Morbidity in Warfare*	*Principal Target Tissue*	*Medical Countermeasures*
Choking (e.g., phosgene)	10%[a]	Airway	Nonspecific; symptomatic treatment
Blood (e.g., cyanide)	Unknown[b]	Cellular respiratory enzymes	Sodium nitrate, sodium thiosulfate
Blister and vesicant agents (e.g., "mustard gas")	2.2%[c]	Skin, airway	Nonspecific; symptomatic treatment
Nerve (e.g., sarin)	Unknown[d]	Central nervous system, neuromuscular transmission	Atropine, oxime, anticonvulsants

Note. From "Psychological Factors in Chemical Warfare and Terrorism" (pp. 398, 401), by J. Romano and J. King, in *Chemical Warfare Agents: Toxicity at Low Levels,* edited by S. Somani and J. Romano, 2001, Boca Raton, FL: CRC Press. Adapted with permission.

[a]World War I figures are estimates because phosgene was often mixed with chlorine. Total personnel injured directly attributed to phosgene = 6,834 directly attributed to phosgene; 66 fatalities. [b]No data from wartime use; however, wartime experiences suggest difficulty in achieving militarily effective concentrations unless confirmed to closed spaces. [c]World War I: 2%, with 27,711 U.S. personnel injured. Iran–Iraq War: 45,000 Iran/Iraqi personnel estimated injured. [d]No data from wartime use; however, on March 20, 1995, using a primitive method of dispersal, sarin was released on Tokyo subways, with 5,500 people seeking medical care. Approximately 1,500 had defined symptoms of exposure, and 12 casualties died. Less well known is the fact that, on June 27, 1994, sarin was released in Matsumoto, Japan, with an estimated 471 people exposed to sarin and 7 deaths.

(National Domestic Preparedness Office, 2001; The White House, 1998a, 1998b) populations and facilities.

During World War I (WWI), when choking and blood agents were used, the choking agent phosgene produced a large number of casualties requiring extensive hospitalization. Sciuto, Moran, Narula, Forster, and Romano (2001) indicated that the primary effects of phosgene on military performance are due to its capacity to produce deep lung injury. Sciuto et al. suggested that phosgene may produce a toxic encephalopathy in humans as phosgene decreases O_2 delivery to the central nervous system (CNS) and other body systems, with accompanying behavioral and functional deficits when continuous mental or physical performance is demanded. They also describe some of these behavioral effects as demonstrated in the psychological literature.

Blood agents appeared in WWI within weeks after the initial use of choking agents (often phosgene and chlorine were employed simultaneously) and produced lethal casualties more rapidly. Cyanide in particular is a biochemical poisoning with affinity for CNS tissue (S. Moore & Gates, 1946). Although highly toxic, gradients of CNS effects can be observed either after exposure to lower concentrations or exposure to lethal amounts via the oral or percutaneous routes (Baskin & Brewer, 1997). Baskin and Rockwood (2002/this issue), in their article, "Neurotoxicological and Behavioral Effects of Cyanide and Its Potential Therapies," report that initial signs of CNS excitement, including anxiety and agitation, may progress to signs of CNS depression, such as coma and dilated, unresponsive pupils. In fact, pathological studies from WWI and WWII indicate that residual cyanide lesions are significant only in the case of animals receiving a narrow range of exposures just below the lethal dose. Recovering animals show residual neurological damage, principally in cerebrum and cerebellum (S. Moore & Gates, 1946).

The most effective agent at producing casualties in WWI was so-called mustard gas, or HD. As Smith (2002/this issue) points out in his article, "Vesicant Agents and Antivesicant Medical Countermeasures: Clinical Toxicology and Psychological Implications," mustard produced hundreds of thousands of casualties, even more casualties than were seen with phosgene, who required extensive hospitalization. The pernicious nature of mustard was reinforced in the mid-1980s in the Iran–Iraq War, in which it produced an estimated additional 45,000 casualties from chemical exposure. The major clinical effects of exposure to HD are significant skin, eye, and pulmonary lesions, which are usually nonfatal. The length of hospitalization for these injuries was estimated to be 46 days per casualty during WWI (Joy, 1997) and up to 10 weeks during the Iran–Iraq War (Willems, 1989). Reports of neuropsychiatric effects, such as severe apathy, impaired concentration, and diminished libido, are given a balanced discussion by Smith.

Following WWI, work in Germany progressed on the development of organophosphorus insecticides, leading to identification of a new a class of compounds of extreme toxicity, the nerve agents. This toxicity, and their rapid action, led to their adoption as weapons of warfare. As highly active CNS agents, sublethal exposures to this type of CWA can be expected to produce prominent deficits in behavior and performance. McDonough's (2002/this issue) article, "Performance Impacts of Nerve Agents and Their Pharmacological Countermeasures," provides a review of the toxicological and neurobehavioral effects of exposure to nerve agents and their medical countermeasures, with an emphasis on human reports. A considerable body of literature exists on this topic, and the interested reader is encouraged to use McDonough's review as well as Longo (1966), Karczmar (1984), and Romano, McDonough, Sheridan, and Sidell (2001) as useful starting points. Somewhat less effort has been given to characterizing the effects of low-level exposures to nerve CWAs, perhaps due to the steepness of their toxicity curves (Romano, Penetar, & King, 1985) and the resultant difficulty in determining low-level dosages. Recent concern over the possible sublethal exposure of U.S. armed forces to the nerve agent sarin (GB) during operations following the Gulf War has led to a renewed study of this problem. The reader can identify pertinent ongoing studies and their annual abstract reports on the Internet at http://www.va.gov/resdev/pgrpt00.htm (*Annual Report to Congress: Federally Sponsored Research on Gulf War Veterans' Illnesses for 2000,* April 2001).

Pharmacological or medical countermeasures to these CWAs can produce CNS sequelae, which are discussed briefly in each of the articles in this issue, with due consideration given to demonstrated or potential psychological effects. Of course, those CWAs, like the nerve agents and the blood agents, which have high affinity to CNS tissue, require medical countermeasures that can be expected to produce significant CNS and performance effects. Two areas of interest are highlighted. First, Baskin and Rockwood (2002/this issue) discuss pretreatment for cyanide poisoning by methemoglobin formation, pointing out that it is estimated that methemoglobin levels of 5% to 7% will protect humans against up to 2 times the LD_{50} of cyanide. To put this in perspective, the level of methemoglobin in smokers' blood is 2%. The effects of a level of 5% to 7% of induced methemoglobin on performance need to be evaluated. Second, medical protection from the effects of nerve agents may involve pretreatment with the reversible acetylcholinesterase inhibitor, pyridostigmine, or with biological scavengers targeted at these compounds. The drug pyridostigmine bromide (PB), which is a reversible acetylcholinesterase inhibitor, has been given a considerable amount of scrutiny recently. This attention may stem from its having been used as a pretreatment to protect U.S. armed forces against the potential use of nerve agents by Iraqi forces during the 1991 Persian Gulf War. Its effects on military performance have been reviewed (Dunn, Hackley, & Sidell, 1997), and its potential health consequences in otherwise healthy U.S. forces are described. The reader is directed to http://www.va.gov/resdev/pgrpt00.htm or http://www.gulflink.osd.mil (Office of the Special Assistant for Gulf War Illnesses, 2001). This Web site provides summaries and abstract reports of research projects examining the health effects of PB either alone or due to its interaction with a variety of other compounds. A detailed consideration of the interactions of PB and stressors is available for interested readers (Somani, Husain, & Jagannathan, 2001).

Protection may also involve pretreatment with a biological scavenger. As Cerasoli and Lenz (2002/this issue) point out in their article, "Nerve Agent Bioscavengers: Protection With Reduced Behavioral Effects," this novel approach avoids the side effects associated with the current nerve agent antidotes. Furthermore, the animal data available, pretreatment with a biological scavenger, appears to prevent or significantly alleviate the neurobehavioral effects of the nerve agents. As a result, the level of protection from the neurobehavioral effects of nerve agents is greater than that seen following use of conventional therapy for nerve agents.

One final point about the response to chemical agents on the battlefield or in the homeland concerns the possible presence of stress casualties. These have been variously labeled as cases of "gas hysteria," "gas mania," or "gas neurosis." It is conceivable that widespread confusion leading to panic and the potential mental health disorder could result from fear or from actual use of CWAs. In a recent review in this journal, Stokes and Banderet (1997) reported that the official U.S. Army Medical Department history notes that two such cases occurred for each actual chemical injury. Their analysis suggested several origins for these cases: (a) conversion disorders, (b) mistaking normal physiological stress symptoms for exposure to CWA (despite significant efforts to train soldiers in proper recognition of signs of poisoning), (c) mistaking or magnifying the symptoms of minor illnesses, and (d) deliberate faking or malingering. One might add the possibility of an additional type of self-inflicted wound to this categorization (i.e., the inadvertent or misguided use of antidotal compounds, e.g., atropine and diazepam). Self-administration of two nerve agent antidote autoinjectors can produce headache, restlessness, and fatigue, symptoms that can be aggravated in a tired, dehydrated, or stressed individual.

Had this issue been compiled in the late 1980s, its application and focus would have generally been limited to the protection of deployed U.S. armed forces. We believe that the world has changed. The CWAs and the medical countermeasures discussed in this issue should be considered as threats to deployed and deploying forces, to fixed military installations either overseas or in the continental U.S., and to the American homeland and its population. Moreover, in the last decade the unthinkable has happened: CWAs have been employed against unprotected civilians by terrorists. These events have challenged the civilian medical and mental health systems, along with the associated first-response systems charged with protection of the population (Ohtomi, 1996; Romano & King, 2001). The magnitude and impact of this challenge to the military and civilian medical and mental health care systems is carefully delineated by Jones (1995), Sidell (1997), Stokes and Banderet (1997), and D. H. Moore and Alexander (2001). These works provide a detailed examination of the current approaches to management of CWA casualties and of plans for the public health response. The current world situation requires that we properly prepare for such CWA attacks by ensuring that accurate, up-to-date information on the behavioral, functional, and neurological impacts of the CWAs and their medical countermeasures is available.

This special issue was conceived to complement the work done by Gerald P. Krueger and Louis E. Banderet in 1997 in the special issue of *Military Psychology* on the "Effects of Chemical Protective Clothing on Military Performance." Their issue addresses the physiological and performance effects of protective clothing and is summarized in the preface (Krueger & Banderet, 1997b). Krueger and Banderet (1997a) also presented a short history on the use of chemical weaponry on the battlefield during the last century. The set of articles in this special issue illustrates the methodologies and results of many U.S. military medical research programs on the threats of the chemical agents to the human body, the research on antidotes to counteract those effects, and the resultant effects of both the threat agents and the antidotes on human psychology and behavior.

Because of the obvious medical and biological threats to humans, much of the research cited here was done by multidisciplinary scientists using animal models in studies designed to predict human bodily and behavioral responses to both CWA threats and to the challenges that accompany use of medical prophylactic countermeasures or treatment regimens.

ACKNOWLEDGMENTS

The opinions or assertions contained herein are the private views of the authors and are not to be construed as official or as reflecting the view of the U.S. Army or the U.S. Department of Defense. The authors thank Patricia D. Little for her skillful editorial assistance in preparation of this article. Her excellence in secretarial skills, assistance in compiling accurate tables, and methodical approach to presentation of the reference citations enabled the publication of this material.

REFERENCES

Annual report to Congress: Federally sponsored research on Gulf War veterans' illnesses for 2000. (2001, October). Washington, DC: Department of Veterans Affairs. Retrieved April 4, 2002, from http://www.va.gov/resdev/pgrpt00.htm

Baskin, S., & Brewer, T. (1997). Cyanide poisoning. In F. R. Sidell, E. T. Takafuji, & D. R. Franz (Eds.), *Medical aspects of chemical and biological warfare* (pp. 271–286). Washington, DC: Office of the Surgeon General.

Baskin, S. I., & Rockwood, G. A. (2002/this issue). Neurotoxicological and behavioral effects of cyanide and its potential therapies. *Military Psychology, 14,* 159–177.

Cerasoli, D. M., & Lenz, D. E. (2002/this issue). Nerve agent bioscavengers: Protection with reduced behavioral effects. *Military Psychology, 14,* 121–143.

Chandler, R. W., & Backschies, J. R. (1998). *The new face of war* (pp. 397–406). McLean, VA: AMCODA Press.

Chandler, R. W., & Trees, R. J. (1996). *Tomorrow's war, today's decisions* (pp. 165–204). McLean, VA: AMCODA Press.

Dunn, M. A., Hackley, B. E., & Sidell, F. R. (1997). Pretreatment for nerve agent exposure. In F. R. Sidell, E. T. Takafuji, & D. R. Franz (Eds.), *Medical aspects of chemical and biological warfare* (pp. 181–196). Washington, DC: Office of the Surgeon General.

Jones, F. D. (1995). Neuropsychiatric casualties of nuclear, biological, and chemical warfare. In F. D. Jones, L. R. Sparacino, V. L. Wilcox, J. M. Rothberg, & J. W. Stokes (Eds.), *War psychiatry* (pp. 85–111). Washington, DC: Office of the Surgeon General.

Joy, R. J. T. (1997). Historical aspects of medical defense against chemical warfare. In F. R. Sidell, E. T. Takafuji, & D. R. Franz (Eds.), *Medical aspects of chemical and biological warfare* (pp. 87–109). Washington, DC: Office of the Surgeon General.

Karczmar, A. G. (1984). Acute and long-lasting concentrations of organophosphorus agents. *Fundamental and Applied Toxicology, 44*(2), S1–S17.

Krueger, G. P., & Banderet, L. E. (1997a). Effects of chemical protective clothing on military performance: A review of the issues. *Military Psychology, 9,* 255–286.

Krueger, G. P., & Banderet, L. E. (1997b). Preface to the special issue. *Military Psychology, 9,* 251–253.

Longo, V. G. (1966). Behavioral and electroencephalographic effects of atropine and related compounds. *Pharmacology Review, 18,* 965–966.

McDonough, J. H. (2002/this issue). Performance impacts of nerve agents and their pharmacological countermeasures. *Military Psychology, 14,* 93–119.

Moore, D. H., & Alexander, S. M. (2001). Emergency response to a chemical warfare incident: Domestic preparedness, first response and public health considerations. In S. Somani & J. Romano (Eds.), *Chemical warfare agents: Toxicity at low levels* (pp. 409–435). Boca Raton, FL: CRC Press.

Moore, S., & Gates, M. (1946). Hydrogen cyanide and cyanogen chloride. In *Summary technical report of Division 9, National Defense Research Committee: Vol. 1. Chemical warfare agents and related chemical problems* (Pt. 1–2, pp. 7–16). Washington, DC: National Defense Research Committee.

National Domestic Preparedness Office. (2001). *Blueprint for the National Domestic Preparedness Office.* Washington, DC: Department of Justice, Federal Bureau of Investigation. Retrieved April 4, 2002, from http://www.ndpo.gov

Office of the Special Assistant for Gulf War Illnesses. (2001). Washington, DC: Department of Defense. Retrieved April 4, 2002, from http://www.gulflink.osd.mil

Ohtomi, S. (1996). Medical experience with sarin casualties in Japan. In J. M. King (Ed.), *1996 Medical Defense Bioscience Review Proceedings* (pp. 1182–1190). Aberdeen Proving Ground, MD: U.S. Army Medical Research Institute of Chemical Defense.

Romano, J., & King, J. (2001). Psychological factors in chemical warfare and terrorism. In S. Somani & J. Romano (Eds.), *Chemical warfare agents: Toxicity at low levels* (pp. 393–407). Boca Raton, FL: CRC Press.

Romano, J. A., McDonough, J. H., Sheridan, R., & Sidell, F. (2001). Health effects of low-level exposure to nerve agents. In S. Somani & J. A. Romano (Eds.), *Chemical warfare agents: Toxicity at low levels* (pp. 1–24). Boca Raton, FL: CRC Press.

Romano, J. A., Penetar, D. M., & King, J. M. (1985). A comparison of physostigmine and soman using taste aversion and nociception. *Neurobehavioral Toxicology and Teratology, 7,* 243–249.

Sciuto, A. M., Moran, T. S., Narula, A., Forster, J. S., & Romano, J. A., Jr. (2001). *Disruption of gas exchange following exposure to the chemical threat agent phosgene: Implications for human performance* (Rep. No. USAMRICD TR–01–06). Aberdeen Proving Ground, MD: U.S. Army Medical Research Institute of Chemical Defense.

Sidell, F. R. (1997). Nerve agents. In F. R. Sidell, E. T. Takafuji, & D. R. Franz (Eds.), *Medical aspects of chemical and biological warfare* (pp. 129–179). Washington, DC: Office of the Surgeon General.

Smith, W. J. (2002/this issue). Vesicant agents and antivesicant medical countermeasures: Clinical toxicology and psychological implications. *Military Psychology, 14,* 145–157.

Somani, S. M., Husain, K., & Jagannathan, R. (2001). Pharmacokinetics and pharmacodynamics of carbamates under physical stress. In S. Somani & J. Romano (Eds.), *Chemical warfare agents: Toxicity at low levels* (pp. 145–189). Boca Raton, FL: CRC Press.

Stokes, J. W., & Banderet, L. E. (1997). Psychological aspects of chemical defense and warfare. *Military Psychology, 9,* 395–415.

The White House. (1998a). *Combating terrorism: Presidential Decision Directive 62* [Fact sheet]. Washington, DC: Office of the Press Secretary.

The White House. (1998b). *Protecting American's critical infrastructures: Presidential Decision Directive 63* [Fact sheet]. Washington, DC: Office of the Press Secretary.

Willems, J. (1989). Clinical management of mustard gas casualties. *Annales Medicinal Militaris Belgicae, 3*(Suppl.), 1–6.

MILITARY PSYCHOLOGY, 2002, *14*(2), 93–119

Performance Impacts of Nerve Agents and Their Pharmacological Countermeasures

John H. McDonough
Applied Pharmacology Branch
U.S. Army Medical Research Institute of Chemical Defense
Aberdeen Proving Ground, Maryland

Nerve agents are some of the most toxic compounds known to man and, as suggested by their name, have pronounced effects on central and peripheral nervous system function. In addition, several of the drugs used as pharmacological countermeasures to reverse the potentially life-threatening physiological effects of nerve agents themselves have potent effects on a variety of neurobehavioral functions. This article reviews the toxicological and neurobehavioral effects of exposure to nerve agents and their medical treatment compounds, giving particular emphasis to their impacts on performance and behavior, both immediate and long-term. As such, this review touches on a number of major related topics, primarily pharmacological and toxicological. Where possible, more in-depth discussions of these topics have been cited for the interested reader. The toxicology and pharmacology of the nerve agents and the respective medical treatment drugs are addressed separately, representing distinctly different pharmacological classes of compounds and producing distinctly different effects on the central nervous system and performance. Both animal and human data have been evaluated for this review. Although animal data provide a valuable adjunct to the human reports, the majority of studies cited here describe the effects of these compounds in humans. Where it was thought necessary for clarification or elaboration, animal studies have been cited, but these represent only a small subset of this vast literature.

This article is part of a special issue, "Chemical Warfare and Chemical Terrorism: Psychological and Performance Outcomes," of *Military Psychology*, 2002, *14*(2), 83–177.

Requests for reprints should be sent to Commander, U.S. Army Medical Research Institute of Chemical Defense, ATTN: MRMC–UV–PA/MCDONOUGH, 3100 Ricketts Point Road, Aberdeen Proving Ground, MD 21010–5400. E-mail: john.mcdonough@apg.amedd.army.mil

NERVE AGENTS: AN OVERVIEW

The nerve agents are highly toxic organophosphorous (OP) compounds that are chemically related to some insecticides (parathion, malathion). The four most common nerve agents are tabun (o-ethyl N,N-dimethyl phosphoramidocyanidate; GA), sarin (isopropyl methyl phosphonofluoridate; GB), soman (pinacolyl methyl phosphonofluoridate; GD), and VX (o-ethyl S-2-N,N-diisopropylaminoethyl methyl phosphonofluoridate). These compounds exist as colorless and relatively odorless liquids and are meant for use in weapons systems (shells, rockets, bombs) that are designed to deliver them as aerosols or fine sprays. They exert their toxic effects by inhibiting the cholinesterase (ChE) family of enzymes that includes acetylcholinesterase (AChE), the enzyme that hydrolyzes the neurotransmitter acetylcholine (ACh). Nerve agents bind to the active site of the AChE enzyme, thus preventing it from hydrolyzing ACh. The enzyme is inhibited irreversibly, and the return of esterase activity depends on the synthesis of new enzyme (approximately 1% per day in humans). All agents are highly lipophylic and readily penetrate the central nervous system (CNS). Acetylcholine is the neurotransmitter at the neuromuscular junction of skeletal muscle, the preganglionic nerves of the autonomic nervous system, the postganglionic parasympathetic nerves, as well as muscarinic and nicotinic cholinergic synapses within the CNS. Following exposure and the inhibition of the AChE enzyme, levels of ACh rapidly increase at the various effector sites, resulting in continuous overstimulation. It is this hyperstimulation of the cholinergic system at central and peripherial sites that leads to the toxic signs of poisoning with these compounds. These signs include miosis (constriction of the pupils), increased tracheobronchial secretions, bronchial constriction, laryngospasm, increased sweating, urinary and fecal incontinence, muscle fasciculations, tremor, convulsions or seizures of CNS origin, and loss of respiratory drive from the CNS. The relative prominence and severity of a given toxic sign depend highly on the route and degree of exposure. Ocular and respiratory effects occur rapidly and are most prominent following vapor exposure, whereas localized sweating, muscle fasciculations, and gastrointestinal disturbances are the predominant signs following percutaneous exposures and usually develop in a more protracted fashion. The acute lethal effects of the nerve agents are due to respiratory failure caused by a combination of effects at both central and peripheral levels and are further complicated by copious secretions, muscle fasciculations, and convulsions. Several excellent reference sources provide more detailed discussions of the history, chemistry, physiochemical properties, pharmacology, and toxicology of the nerve agents (Koelle, 1963; Sidell, 1992, 1997; Somani, Solana, & Dube, 1992; Taylor, 1985).

TREATMENT OF NERVE AGENT EXPOSURE

Physical protective measures (e.g., gas masks, gloves, and overgarments; see especially Krueger & Banderet, 1997) and strict decontamination procedures are the most effective means of protection against the toxic action of these agents. If intoxication does occur, treatment of nerve agent poisoning is focused along several lines. Prevention or reduction of the toxic signs is accomplished primarily via the (a) administration of anticholinergic drugs, atropine sulfate being almost universally used for this purpose; (b) reactivation of agent-inhibited enzyme with oxime reactivators such as pralidoxime chloride (2-PAM Cl); and when indicated in cases of severe poisoning (c) treatment of convulsions or seizures with benzodiazepine drugs (*Medical Management of Chemical Casualties Handbook,* 1999; Sidell, 1974, 1992, 1997).

Anticholinergic drugs such as atropine block the action of ACh overstimulation at central and peripheral muscarinic sites. As such, it provides symptomatic relief of the excessive secretory responses, laryngospasm, and to a lesser extent, the loss of central respiratory drive, but it is unable to counteract the nicotinic signs of intoxication. Reversal of the nicotinic signs of intoxication is performed primarily via oxime reactivation of inhibited enzyme. Like other OP anti-ChE compounds, the nerve agents react with AChE by phosphylating the active site of the enzyme. Oximes are nucleophilic compounds that are capable of splitting off the phosphorus atom from the active site, thereby restoring enzyme activity. However, oxime treatment of a nerve agent casualty is complicated by several factors.

First, the ability of a given oxime to reactivate nerve agent-inhibited enzyme is highly dependent on the specific nerve agent, owing to individual differences in the structures of the enzyme-inhibitor complex. Second, the phosphylated enzyme can undergo a dealkylation reaction, termed *aging*, that makes the resultant enzyme-inhibitor complex totally resistant to oxime reactivation. The different agents vary considerably in their rates of aging, with soman (GD) being the fastest (minutes) and the others considerably slower (hours). Third, oximes are quaternary drugs, do not penetrate the blood brain barrier, and thus provide minimal reactivation of CNS-inhibited enzyme. For these reasons, no single oxime has been developed that provides equivalent therapeutic efficacy against all nerve agents (Dawson, 1994).

Treatment of nerve agent-induced convulsions is essential for overall casualty management and reducing the potential for subsequent brain damage that could result from the prolonged seizure activity (McDonough & Shih, 1997). Benzodiazepine drugs such as diazepam are most commonly used to antagonize nerve agent-induced seizures.

Because nerve agents can produce rapid lethal effects, U.S. military personnel are issued several different automatic injector devices to deliver drugs intramuscularly (IM) for immediate emergency treatment in the event of nerve agent exposure. Individuals are issued three MARK 1 treatment drug kits; each kit contains two autoinjectors, one with 2 mg of atropine and the other with 600 mg of the oxime 2-PAM Cl. Individuals are also issued an autoinjector containing 10 mg of diazepam, providing each soldier with a total of up to 6 mg of atropine, 1,800 mg of 2-PAM Cl, and 10 mg of diazepam. The rationale and guidelines for the use of these treatment drugs are based on the route and severity of poisoning and have been discussed in detail elsewhere (*Medical Management of Chemical Casualties Handbook,* 1999; Sidell, 1992, 1997). It should be noted that other countries have a different complement of drugs for treating nerve agent casualties, but the differences are more in the specific drug used rather than in the general treatment approach itself (Moore, Clifford, Crawford, Cole, & Baggett, 1995). Virtually all countries use atropine as the anticholinergic treatment compound and diazepam, or a water-soluble prodrug form (Avizafone), as the benzodiazepine. The greatest difference involves the choice of oxime treatment. The United States and France use the chloride salt (2-PAM Cl) of the mono-oxime, praldoxime, whereas the United Kingdom uses the sulfonate salt (referred to as P2S). Other countries favor a more potent bisquaternary oxime, such as obidoxime (Toxogonin) or TMB-4 (Trimedoxime).

In addition to the drugs used to treat the signs and symptoms of acute intoxication, U.S. military personnel also have a pretreatment drug, pyridostigmine bromide (PB), that is to be taken prophylactically when the threat of use of certain nerve agents is considered high (Dunn, Hackley, & Sidell, 1997). PB is a carbamate drug that is a spontaneously reactivating inhibitor of ChE, which attaches to the same site on the enzyme as the nerve agent, but this attachment is only temporary. This binding by PB prevents the binding of nerve agents and thus temporarily shields the enzyme from irreversible inhibition by the nerve agent. In practice, doses of PB are given that are targeted to inhibit approximately 20% to 30% of the total pool of ChE in the body. This reversible carbamylation protects a fraction of the enzyme pool, and spontaneous decarbamylation of this enzyme fraction following exposure, along with rapid removal of excess OP from the body, will provide sufficient enzyme to then degrade the excess ACh. PB pretreatment is especially beneficial when (a) the agents are resistant to reactivation with the treatment oxime (2-PAM Cl is the only oxime approved for clinical use in the United States, and it has poor reactivating properties against tabun [GA] or soman [GD] inhibited enzyme), or (b) the agent used ages so rapidly (e.g., soman) that there is minimal time for oxime treatment. It should be noted that PB pretreatment does not obviate the need for standard therapy treatment after exposure. Prompt postexposure administration of atropine is still needed to antagonize ACh excess, and an oxime reactivator must also be given if an excess of nerve agent remains to attack the newly uncovered AChE active sites that were protected by pyridostigmine. PB is provided to military personnel in the form of 30 mg tablets, in a 21-tablet blister pack (the nerve agent pyridostigmine pretreatment set; NAPPS), with only one tablet to be taken every 8 hr. Doses are not to be doubled up in the case of a missed dose because this may lead to excessive AChE inhibition. The use of PB pretreatment is to be a command decision made at division level or above, based on assessment of the chemical agent threat by chemical, intelligence, and medical staff officers. Current U.S. military doctrine calls for a maximum pretreatment period of 21 days, with frequent reassessments of the need for continued pretreatment.

It should be noted that the treatment of nerve agent exposure in a military setting poses a unique medical problem: Individuals who are medically naive must accurately diagnose the signs and symptoms of a potentially lethal exposure and then administer to themselves or their fellow soldier the necessary treatment drugs in the proper order and the proper dosage. This is of special concern due to the need for prompt antidote administration by the individual soldier who is given a complement of drugs that by themselves have potent effects on behavior and performance.

A major issue in this regard is dose-response. There are low doses of nerve agent, and likewise of the various pretreatment and antidote compounds, that produce minimal to mild signs or symptoms of the agent or compound's effect. For example, the ocular effects of nerve agents, which will be discussed in more detail, occur at very low exposure levels and may be the only physical sign of exposure. At higher doses, these effects may be magnified in degree and duration and become part of a constellation of the effect of the agent or drug on other organ systems. Thus, the magnitude and duration of a particular physiological effect is highly dependent on the level of agent exposure or dose of drug.

NERVE AGENT EFFECTS

The signs and symptoms of nerve agent exposure involve the following organs or organ systems: eye, nose, mouth, pulmonary tract, gastrointestinal tract, sweat glands, muscular system, and CNS. Details of the physiological effects of nerve agents on these organs or organ systems, as well as on performance, have been extensively reviewed by Sidell (1992, 1996, 1997), and the following account draws heavily on these sources. Some of the signs and symptoms of nerve agent exposure have features similar to other psychological clinical conditions that may be manifested in military situations. For example, anxiety states such as panic disorder have several clinical symptoms (e.g., dyspena, chest pain or discomfort, choking or smothering sensations, sweating, and trembling) that are similar to some symptoms of mild to moderate nerve agent exposure. Indeed, such signs of acute panic disorder may have contributed to the many individuals in the Tokyo subway terrorist attack that had self-reported physical complaints, yet displayed no clinical sign of nerve agent exposure. Likewise, some of the symptoms indicative of posttraumatic stress disorder (PTSD; e.g., sleep disturbance, memory impairment, or trouble concentrating) are among the neurobehavioral effects also reported to occur following moderate to severe exposure to a nerve agent. Following are ways that a differential diagnosis can be made between immediate or long-term effects arising from true nerve agent exposures and these other psychological conditions.

Eye

The effects of nerve agents on the eye include miosis, conjunctival injection, pain in or around the eye, and dim or blurred vision. These effects are most prominent following vapor, aerosol, or direct liquid exposure, but can also occur following systemic (percutaneous, oral) exposure usually as a delayed effect (Nozaki et al., 1995). Miosis (contraction of the pupil) can occur rapidly following vapor exposure but may not be maximal for an hour or so if the concentration is low. Miosis was the most common medical effect of the exposure to sarin in the 1994 Matsumoto and 1995 Tokyo subway terrorist attacks in Japan, and in the majority of cases, it was the only physical sign of exposure (Kato & Hamanaka, 1996; Masuda, Takatsu, Morinari, & Ozawa, 1995; Morita et al., 1995; Ohbu et al., 1997; Okumura et al., 1996). Because miosis is a result of a local effect on pupillary muscles, unilateral miosis can occur in cases in which exposure is restricted to one eye, which, in turn, can cause difficulty with depth perception (the Pulfrich stereo effect; Hayes, 1982). The duration of miosis varies depending on the degree of exposure; the pupils may react normally outdoors or in bright light within several days of exposure, but the ability to fully dilate in darkness may not return for 6 to 9 weeks (Rengstorff, 1985; Sidell, 1974).

Dim vision following nerve agent exposure is generally thought to be a result of the reduced amount of light reaching the retina due to miosis. In keeping with this, Stewart, Madill, and Dyer (1968) reported that the reduction in pupil size correlated with the reduction in visual sensitivity following instillation of sarin on the eyeball. However, other evidence suggests that dim vision is a central (at the retina or other level of CNS) effect of exposure. For example, Craig and Freeman (1953) reported that, in workers accidentally exposed to "G" agents, the degree of dim vision began to recover before objective changes in miosis (pupil diameter) occurred, and Rubin, Krop, and Goldberg (1957) showed that dim vision was not present when miosis was produced by direct application of a nerve agent to the eye. Conversely, Rubin and Goldberg (1958) then showed that dim vision could be produced in the absence of miosis following systemic administration of sarin. Furthermore, the reduction in visual threshold could be reversed by atropine sulfate, which enters the CNS, but not by atropine methyl nitrate, which acts only peripherially; neither drug altered pupil size (Rubin & Goldberg, 1958).

Miosis and reduction in visual sensitivity will therefore significantly impact the performance of individuals who depend on accurate vision in a dim light. Human exposure studies, detailed by Sidell (1996), in general note that night operations would be severely compromised by exposures that only produce miosis. Driving a vehicle in the early evening or at night, monitoring a tracking or computer screen in dim light, and night operations in the field are but a few examples of military activities that could be seriously compromised by miosis and a reduction in visual sensitivity produced by nerve agent exposure. These effects can occur at levels of exposure that do not produce life-threatening toxic signs and may persist for at least several days.

Pain in and around the eye is another symptom that is commonly reported following vapor exposure. For example, in the Tokyo subway terrorist incident, 45% to 55% of the victims reported eye pain (Kato & Hamanaka, 1996; Ohbu et al., 1997; Okumura et al., 1996). The pain is due to ciliary spasm and can become significantly worse when the victim looks at a bright light (Sidell, 1997). Local instillation of an anticholinergic drug (atropine, homatropine) can relieve the pain, but because this, in turn, causes blurred vision due to a paralysis of the ciliary muscles (Moylan-Jones & Thomas, 1973; Nozaki & Aikawa, 1995), this treatment has been recommended only in cases of severe pain.

It is worth noting that the previously listed ocular signs of nerve agent exposure are not seen in states of extreme anxiety or panic.

Nose

Rhinorrhea (the free discharge of thin nasal mucus) is another common sign of exposure to nerve agent vapor and may precede or occur even in the absence of miosis (Sidell, 1992, 1997). Such rhinorrhea can be quite pronounced and has been compared with the flow from a leaking faucet. Although rhinorrhea occurs as part of a generalized increase in secretions from glands (salivary, pulmonary, gastrointestinal) following severe exposure by any route, it becomes a concern only with regard to how the secretions may interfere with respiration or protective mask integrity. Rhinorrhea is not among the signs that characterize anxiety or panic.

Gastrointestinal System

Nerve agents also cause an increase in the motility of the gastrointestinal tract and an increase in the secretions of the glands in the wall of the gastrointestinal tract. Nausea, vomiting, and diarrhea are common signs following percutaneous or oral exposure (Sidell, 1974, 1992). For example, nausea and vomiting were notable symptoms (60% and 37%, respectively) following moderate or severe vapor exposures in the Tokyo incident, but diarrhea was significantly less evident (5%; Okumura et al., 1996). Upset stomach, frequent urination, and diarrhea are also noted as symptomatic of generalized anxiety. Perhaps the key features to make a differential diagnosis on the basis of these symptoms are their frequency, intensity, and proximity of presentation relative to the suspected agent exposure.

Pulmonary System

A "tight chest" or shortness of breath is another typical complaint following exposure to small amounts of nerve agent vapor. Dyspnea (difficult or labored breathing) is generally attributed to spasm or constriction of the bronchiolar musculature and is also accompanied by increased bronchial secretions; the effect depends on the concentration and dose. Following high-dose exposures, respiration rapidly becomes gasping and irregular, and the victim can become cyanotic and totally apneic in a severe poisoning (Sidell, 1974, 1992, 1997). These effects may be substantially delayed in onset after percutaneous exposures. If the exposure is small, dyspnea may begin to resolve spontaneously in 15 to 30 min following removal from the contaminated atomosphere and require no further treatment. However, if the exposure is larger, only therapeutic administration of an anticholinergic such as atropine will provide relief from these potentially life-threatening signs. Rescue breathing or attempts to mechanically aid respiration in a severely poisoned casuality may be greatly hampered by secretions and constriction of the bronchiolar musculature. Death from nerve agent poisoning is generally from respiratory failure, which has been shown in animal studies to occur before circulatory failure (Rickett, Glenn, & Beers, 1986; Wright, 1954). Bronchosecretions, bronchoconstriction, muscular weakness, and a loss of central respiratory drive all contribute to respiratory failure, although loss of central respiratory drive is probably the most critical element (DeCandole et al., 1953; Rickett et al., 1986; Wright, 1954). Dyspenia, chest pains or discomfort, choking or smothering sensations are also signs in acute panic attacks. Keeping the patient quiet, ongoing visual monitoring of respiratory status and oxygenation, as well as the presence or absence of other signs of nerve agent intoxication can serve as guidelines for differential diagnosis and treatment.

Skeletal Muscle

The effects of nerve agents on the skeletal muscles begin as stimulation at muscle fibers and then progress to stimulation of individual muscles and muscle groups. This is later followed by fatigue and paralysis of these areas. The effects are characterized by fasciculations, muscle twitches or jerks, and fatigue. Fasciculations are involuntary visible contractions of muscle fibers innervated by a single motor nerve filament and appear as random ripples under the skin. They can occur as a local effect in response to absorption of the nerve agent through the skin or in many muscle groups throughout the body in response to a large systemic exposure. Fasciculations can persist for several days following a large exposure even when other symptoms have subsided.

Muscle twitches or jerks are sudden and intense contractions of muscle groups and occur following large exposures. The limbs may flail about, or the limbs and torso may show rigid hyperextention. These motor movements have been described as convulsive jerks, but animal studies show they can occur in the absence of brain epileptiform activity (Shih, McDonough, & Koplovitz, 1999). Occasionally, these disturbances may be a local response of the muscle groups near the site of exposure, such as the marked trismus and nuchal rigidity of a man who accidently pipetted soman into his mouth (Sidell, 1974). Following several minutes of this intense hyperactivity, the muscles become fatigued and a seeming flacid paralysis occurs. In extreme anxiety, muscle tension and shaking or trembling can be common symptoms. However, the involuntary nature of the effects of nerve agents on skeletal muscle, especially fasciculations, are unmistakable and can serve to distinguish between severe anxiety and mild or moderate nerve agent exposure.

Central Nervous System and Behavior

The behavioral effects of exposure to nerve agents or other potent OP compounds in humans have been described in a number of reports over the years that generally divide the behavioral and CNS symptoms of nerve agent exposure into three classes: effects on cognitive processes, effects on mood or affect, and disturbances of sleep–wakefulness. Perhaps the best and most thorough examples of clinical descriptions of the behavioral syndrome associated with nerve agent and OP compound exposure were given by Grob and his associates (Grob & Harvey, 1953, 1958; Grob, Harvey, Langworthy, & Lilenthal, 1947). In these studies, human volunteers were administered di-isopropyl fluorophosphate (DFP; Grob et al., 1947) or sarin (Grob & Harvey, 1953, 1958), and the development of CNS and behavioral signs of exposure were monitored and related to degree of ChE depression. The major CNS and behavioral effects noted in both studies were excessive dreaming, insomnia, increased fatigue and weakness, restlessness (the terms *tension, jitteriness,* and *anxiety* are also commonly used in these reports but without a precise distinction as to the subjective symptom to which they refer), tremulousness, depression, and a difficulty in concentrating or mental confusion. Similar effects have been noted in workers accidentally exposed to small amounts of nerve agent vapor (cited by Sidell, 1992, 1996, 1997) following percutaneous nerve agent exposure (VX) in human volunteers (Bowers, Goodman, & Sim, 1964) or individuals exposed by a variety of routes to OP insecticides (Holmes & Gaon, 1956). These effects can develop usually a few hours after exposure and may last from several days to several weeks depending on severity of exposure. In the case of severe exposures, these behavioral changes become notable following recovery from the acute toxic effects (see Sidell, 1974, for an excellent description of such cases) and again may last from several days to several weeks depending on the severity of exposure.

Although blood ChE data are lacking in some reports, overall the studies indicate a standard dose–effect relation; there are increased percentages of individuals affected, and the number, intensity, and duration of behavioral effects are proportional to the magnitude of blood ChE inhibition. In the Grob and Harvey (1958) study, behavioral symptoms of exposure began usually coincident with the depression of red blood cell ChE to 22% of original values (78% inhibited) following single oral doses of sarin, but if the dose were given intravascularly (in which effects of the agent occur very rapidly), symptoms could occur with as little as 50% inhibition of red blood cell ChE. However, under conditions of smaller, repeated, oral doses (mimicking the conditions of chronic, low-level exposures), there was no correlation between the onset of symptoms and the precise level of ChE activity except that ChE was inhibited 78% or more when symptoms were experienced. These data highlight an important fact: The rate at which ChE is inhibited by the nerve agent is a major factor in determining the expression of symptoms. Rapid inhibition of ChE may produce symptoms and CNS effects at lower exposure levels, whereas slower, more protracted exposures may result in greater levels of ChE inhibition with minimal effects being manifested (see Sidell, 1997, pp. 138–139, for a more thorough discussion about ChE inhibition and relation to signs and symptoms). In their study with acute percutaneous exposures to VX, Bowers et al. (1964) reported that CNS and behavioral symptoms occurred at ChE inhibition levels of 70% (30% of normal), which is in close agreement with the figures sited by Grob and Harvey. In summary, behavioral and CNS symptoms of exposure have not been seen at levels of ChE inhibition less than 50% and are more typically seen when inhibition levels are equal to or greater than 70% to 80% of normal levels.

The effect on cognitive processes can best be described as a general intellectual slowing. There are concentration and memory retention difficulties, a loss of subject matter and thought trends in conversations, poor performance on simple arithmetic problems, decreased ability to communicate, and minor disturbances in orientation, yet individuals retain insight to the fact that they are decremented. Illogical or inappropriate thinking and responses, as well as perceptual distortions or hallucinations, are not seen. The effects on mood and affect, which are commonly reported following nerve agent exposure as depression, anxiety, and irritation, are noted during both the acute phase (hours to days) immediately following a mild to moderate exposure and as a common complaint during recovery (lasting weeks to months) of individuals who have experienced severe exposures. Likewise, disturbances of sleep–wakefulness are also consistently reported to occur following exposures to nerve agents. The two most frequent, and seemingly paradoxical, complaints are insomnia and increased dreaming. Both effects appear to be most prominent immediately following the exposure and then lessen. How much the insomnia may be due to other physical disturbances (e.g., jitteriness, restlessness, or nausea) brought about by the nerve agent is difficult to determine from reports. The increase in dreaming is also quite dramatic. The dreams occur more frequently, begin earlier in the sleep cycle than normal, and are reported both as vivid and with frightening content.

This cluster of CNS and behavioral effects of nerve agents is consistent with what is known about the role of acetylcholine and cholinergic neurons within the brain. Central cholinergic circuits are involved in both cognition and short-term memory, as demonstrated by the effects of drugs (Brimblecombe, 1974), experimentally produced lesions (Voytko, 1996), and naturally occurring pathological states of cholinergic insufficiency such as Alzheimer's disease (Bartus, Dean, Beer, & Lippa, 1982). In addition, it has been hypothesized for a number of years that depression is due to an imbalance between the cholinergic and adrenergic systems within the brain, and that depressive symptoms are associated with cholinergic hyperactivity (Davis, Berger, Hollister, & Barchas, 1978; Janowsky & Overstreet, 1990; Janowsky, Risch, & Gillin, 1983). Finally, sleep cycle control, specifically the initiation and maintenance of the rapid eye movement (REM) stage of sleep, the sleep stage that is associated with dreaming, is controlled by increased activity of cholinergic neurons within specific nuclei in the pontine brain stem (Baghdoyan et al., 1984; George, Haslett, & Jenden, 1964; Gnadt & Pegram, 1986; Hobson, 1992). Administration of carbamates, OP anticholinesterase compounds, or cholinergic agonists that act like nerve agents can induce REM sleep in both animals and humans (Gillin, Sitram, Mendelson, & Wyatt, 1978; Gnadt, Atwood, Meighen, & Pegram, 1986; Gnadt, Pegram, & Baxter, 1985; Hobson, 1992; Sitram, Wyatt, Dawson, & Gillin, 1976).

It is notable that many of the immediate and long-lasting effects of nerve agents on CNS and behavior have symptoms that are also seen in extreme anxiety, depressive disorders, and PTSD. Indeed, as discussed previously, at least one of these psychological states has a biological basis in the cholinergic system. A suspected or documented exposure to a nerve agent that elicited some of the clinical signs described previously, as well as a confirmed depression of blood ChE levels below standard values, would be the key diagnostic factors to distinguish between a toxicological versus psychological basis for such complaints.

Electroencephalogram

In conjunction with their action on the CNS and behavior, the nerve agents also produce concurrent effects on the electroencephalographic (EEG) activity of the brain. Glenn, Hinman, and McMaster (1987) reviewed the effects of various anticholinesterase agents (nerve agents, other OP compounds, and carbamates) on EEG activity and have proposed that a three-stage change is produced in the normal EEG of animals or humans by progressively higher doses of these compounds. At Stage I, an activation pattern is produced in the EEG, which is characterized by a low amplitude desynchronized pattern of mixed frequencies normally seen in alert subjects. This pattern is induced regardless of the subject's behavioral state when the anticholinesterase is administered and may last from minuets to several hours depending on the dose and the type of compound. This Stage I pattern is associated with an approximately 30% to 60% inhibition of RBC ChE, which would be comparable to levels of inhibition associated with minimal to mild signs or symptoms of exposure. It can be conjectured that this level of ChE inhibition may also be associated with some mild, short-term, effect on REM sleep.

The Stage II EEG pattern is marked by a continuation of the activation pattern seen during Stage I, with intrusions of high-voltage, slow-frequency (delta, theta) waves and an increased amount of high frequency (beta) waves. The Stage II pattern is associated with mild to moderate signs or symptoms of intoxication in both human and animal studies. These EEG changes may persist for hours or days depending on the severity of the dose and are associated with approximately 60% to 80% inhibition of ChE. Such levels of exposure would also be expected to produce a moderate increase of REM.

Stage III EEG changes are associated with the most severe levels of exposure and are represented by epileptiform activity in a variety of patterns. Most typically, this is marked by very high-voltage waves, with low-frequency delta waves being most prominent. There are marked signs of agent intoxication as well as seizure and convulsive activity that requires immediate pharmacological treatment. Following such severe exposures, EEG changes may be prominent for months to years depending on the severity of the initial insult and possibly on the rapidity and effectiveness of pharmacological treatment. Long-term EEG effects show up as isolated spikes, or sharp waves, or both during sleep or drowsiness, or with hyperventilation (Grob et al., 1947; Grob & Harvey, 1958; Holmes & Gaon, 1956; Metcalf & Holmes, 1969; Sekijima et al., 1995). Such severe EEG and neurobehavioral effects are associated with levels of ChE inhibition greater than 70%. The effects of such severe exposures on REM sleep are quite prominent and can persist for weeks or months after the exposure. In animal experimental studies, unchecked nerve agent-induced seizures can persist over a period of many hours and can result in brain damage and long-term neurobehavioral changes; both the brain damage and neurobehavioral effects can be blocked or minimized by rapid treatment with appropriate anticonvulsant drugs (McDonough & Shih, 1997; Shih, Koviak, & Capacio, 1991; Shih & McDonough, 1997). Such brain damage has not been documented in humans as a result of exposure following severe poisoning with either nerve agents or OP pesticides.

Long-Term Neurobehavioral Effects of Nerve Agent Exposure

There has been continuing concern over the years that an acute, symptomatic, exposure to nerve agents or OP pesticides may produce long-term changes in brain function and behavior. This concern is no doubt brought on by the relatively long-lasting neurobehavioral changes that occur following a severe acute exposure. Metcalf and Holmes (1969) descriptively summarized their findings of workers who had been accidentally exposed during the manufacturing process of nerve agents or OP pesticides at Rocky Mountain Arsenal. They reported that the workers' EEGs showed higher voltage with more pronounced alpha rhythm and bursts of theta activity in light drowsiness. All-night sleep recordings indicated a higher percentage of "narcoleptic" sleep patterns marked by early REM periods. These workers also complained of minor memory problems and difficulty in maintaining alertness and focusing attention. This report led to a more formal study of this worker population by Duffy, Burchfiel, Bartels, Gaon, and Sim (1979), in which workers with documented symptomatic exposures to the nerve agent sarin, at least 1 year before EEG examination, were evaluated against a control group. They found that exposed workers had increased high-frequency beta activity, increased amounts of slow (delta, theta) activity with nonspecific background EEG abnormalities in the resting EEG, and increased amounts of REM sleep. These effects were most prominent in workers who had experienced multiple symptomatic exposures. In a study that resulted in similar findings by Burchfiel, Duffy, and Sim (1976) in nonhuman primates exposed to sarin, rhesus monkeys were exposed to a single high dose of sarin that elicited signs of a severe acute poisoning. Another group of monkeys in the study received a series (one injection per week for 10 weeks) of lower doses of sarin that elicited minimal signs of intoxication. Increased amounts of high frequency beta activity were seen in animals in both exposure conditions, and these changes persisted for a year.

Epidemiological studies of OP-pesticide-poisoned humans have also been performed. A study by Savage et al. (1988) retrospectively examined 100 individuals with documented acute OP pesticide poisoning and compared them with matched-pair nonpoisoned controls. They reported no differences between the two groups in visually inspected EEGs or in a number of neurological tests. There were, however, significant differences between the two groups in their performance on a number of neuropsychological tests, as well as self- and family-assessment of functioning ratings. Their results showed subtle long-term neuropsychological sequelae to acute OP poisoning that are difficult to detect with standard neurological exams that stress sensory and motor function. More recently, Rosenstock, Keifer, Daniell, McConnell, and Claypoole (1991) performed a retrospective neuropsychological study of OP-poisoned agricultural workers and compared them with a matched control group. They found that, when tested 2 years after exposure, poisoned workers self-reported significantly higher numbers of neuropsychological difficulties and had significantly lower test scores than controls on tests of verbal attention, visual memory, and visuomotor and motor functions, as well as tests of visuomotor sequencing and problem solving.

In the several terrorist uses of nerve agents in Japan, amnesia has been reported as a sequala in two very severe cases of poisoning, which may possibly be attributed to severe hypoxia experienced during the acute intoxication (Hatta, Miura, Asukai, & Harnabe, 1996; Nozaki et al., 1995). Another severely poisoned individual has displayed persistent epileptiform discharges in the sleep EEG for up to 1 year following the poisoning (Sekijima et al., 1995). More recently, Yokoyama et al. (1998a, 1998b) evaluated potential prolonged neurobehavioral and neurophysiological consequences of victims of the sarin poisoning in the Tokyo subway. Eighteen sarin-exposed patients (9 men and 9 women) were evaluated (neurobehavioral tests, PTSD checklist, visual- and auditory-evoked potentials, and computerized static posturography) 6 to 8 months following poisoning and compared with a matched control group. Scores on the digit symbol test (psychomotor performance) were significantly lower in sarin cases than in controls. Sarin cases also had higher scores on a general health questionnaire (GHQ) of psychiatric symptoms, the fatigue scale of the Profile of Moods States (POMS), and the PTSD checklist. The scores on the GHQ and fatigue (POMS) scale were positively correlated with the PTSD scores in the sarin cases. On the neurophysiological tests, the latency of the P300 component of the event-related potential and the P100 latency of the visual-evoked potential were significantly longer than controls. Sarin-exposed women also had a significant increase in low-frequency postural sway than did exposed men or those in the control group. Similar neuropsychological or neurophysiological studies of sarin-exposed victims in the Matsumoto terrorist attack have not been done, but in a survey 1 year after that incident, some victims still complained of fatigue, asthenopia (weakness or easy fatigue of the visual organs), dimness of vision, and a general loss of strength (Nakajima et al., 1997).

There has also been concern that low-level exposure to nerve agents or OP pesticides, at levels that produce minimal or no clinical symptoms of intoxication, will produce a long-term change in neurobehavioral function. In the Burchfiel et al. (1976) study, one group of monkeys ($n = 3$) received repeated low doses (1 per week for 10 weeks) of sarin and remained asymptomatic throughout the whole exposure period but displayed similar EEG increases in beta activity as the symptomatic high-dose group. In another study, Korsak and Sato (1977) reported that OP pesticide workers with relatively high occupational levels of exposure to OP pesticides, in comparison with workers with low levels of exposure, tended to have increased EEG power within the beta frequencies, primarily in frontal areas of the brain. In addition, the high-exposure level group had lower performance on a Trail Making Test and the Bender Visual Motor Gestalt test. The authors suggested that these results indicated subtle frontal lobe dysfunction in the exposed subjects. In contrast, Ames, Steenland, Jenkins, Chrislop, and Russo (1995) studied professional pesticide application workers who had at least one documented case of ChE inhibition but no symptoms of exposure. They were compared with a group of controls, and no differences were detected in central or peripheral nervous system function. Stokes, Stark, Marshall, and Narang (1995) also studied similar pesticide workers during the off-season and found a significant decrease in their vibrotactile sensitivity when compared to a matched control group. In another study, Stephens et al. (1995) compared the neuropsychological performance of sheep farmers who had been occupationally exposed to OP pesticides during the course of sheep dipping with a nonexposed matched control group. The farmers performed significantly worse than controls in tests to assess sustained attention and speed of information processing; short-term memory and learning abilities were no different between the groups.

It is clear from the previous review that exposure to doses of nerve agents or OP pesticides that produce overt toxic effects can result in subtle long-term changes in the resting EEG as well as a modest reduction in performance on neuropsychological tests that measure sustained attention, memory, and mood. These changes are evident long after the resolution of clinical signs and the recovery of blood and tissue ChE to normal levels and appear to be very subtle because they are not detected by standard clinical neurological examinations. The consequences of these changes on quality of life or day-to-day functioning, either intellectually or emotionally, appear to be small if not negligible (National Research Council, 1982). At present, there is no convincing evidence that levels of nerve agents or OP exposure that are asymptomatic and produce minimal changes in ChE are capable of producing any significant acute or long-term neurobehavioral effects.

EFFECTS OF MEDICAL COUNTERMEASURES

Atropine

The neurobehavioral effects of atropine have been reviewed by Longo (1966), Headley (1982) and Penetar (1990), and the following account draws heavily from those excellent sources. Atropine has prominent effects on heart rate, thermoregulation, vision, and cognitive processes. In the doses carried by the individual soldier for use as emergency treatment, three 2-mg injectors (6 mg total) of atropine can produce pronounced effects on all of those functions.

The vagus nerve acts to decelerate heart rate via a cholinergic input to the sinoatrial node, and atropine blocks this action, leading to an increase in heart rate. Effects are noted at doses as low as 0.6 mg per 70 kg of body weight, and the maximum increase of 35 to 50 beats per min is achieved at doses of 2 to 3 mg per 70 kg of body weight. Heart rate begins to increase within 15 min of an IM injection, peaks at 60 to 90 min, and can persist for 4 hr (Penetar, 1990; Penetar, Haegerstrom-Portnoy, & Jones, 1988).

Atropine also inhibits salivation, bronchial secretions, and sweating. These effects occur over the same dose range and with a similar time-course as the cardiac effects. The inhibition of sweating can have potentially serious consequences on performance because performing even moderate amounts of work in a warm environment or in chemical protective gear puts the individual at serious risk from heat injury due to the inability to regulate core temperature. For example, Sidell (1992) cited a study in which more than half of 35 soldiers were unable to complete an approximately 6.5 mile hike within 115 min in 83 °F weather after receiving 2 mg (IM) of atropine due to sustaining core temperatures of 103.5 °F; the same march was successfully completed by all soldiers in the absence of atropine. Similar decrements in physical performance were noted following doses of only 2 mg of atropine in several of the older studies reviewed by Headley (1982). More recently, Kobrick, Johnson, and McMenemy (1990) tested the effects of 2 mg of atropine plus 600 mg of 2-PAM Cl (IM) on a number of militarily relevant psychological tasks in volunteers while they were wearing the standard battle dress uniform (BDU) or full chemical protective clothing (Military Oriented Protective Posture [MOPP] Level IV) under two heat–humidity conditions (75 °F/30% relative humidity vs. 95 °F/60% relative humidity). All BDU heat sessions with atropine were completed (6 hr) with some task impairments and a few subjective reactions. In contrast, MOPP-IV heat sessions with atropine could not be continued beyond 2 hr; all tasks were impaired, and subjective reactions were numerous and severe.

Cholinergic innervation of the eye controls the ciliary muscles of the lens and the sphincter muscle of the iris. Blockade of this activity with atropine produced paralysis of the ciliary muscle (cycloplegia) and pupil dilation (mydriasis). Two studies show a dose-related increase of 1 to 2 mm in pupil size following IM administration of 2 to 4 mg in humans (Baker et al., 1983; Haegerstrom-Portnoy, Jones, Adams, & Jampolsky, 1987). Although onset of the effect is slow (40 to 60 min) and can continue for 6 hr, dilated pupils are still evident 24 hr after administration (Penetar et al., 1988). The paralysis of the ciliary muscle results in the loss of accommodation and near vision, and near visual acuity can be degraded for up to 24 hr following a 4-mg dose (Penetar et al., 1988). In addition, there is degradation in eye–hand tracking with 2- or 4-mg doses of atropine (Penetar & Beatrice, 1986). It was noted in all these studies that the effects on accommodation would be accentuated in older personnel (over 35 years) in which near-focusing ability is already degraded due to aging.

Atropine can also have marked effects on cognitive functions, particularly short-term memory. These effects are prominent with doses greater than 4 mg and become notable 40 min after IM dosing, peak at 60 to 90 min, and then wane over 3 to 12 hr depending on the dose (Ketchum, Sidell, Crowell, Aghajanian, & Hayes, 1973; Moylan-Jones, 1969). Both animal and human studies show that it is the storage of new information and its immediate recall that is affected by atropine (Higgins, Woodward, & Henningfield, 1989; Ketchum et al., 1973; Mewaldt & Ghoneim, 1979; Penetar & McDonough, 1983; Wetherell, 1980). The Wetherell study reported effects on digit span at doses as low as 2 mg, but these effects were slight and did not last long. Pickworth, Herning, Koeppl, and Henningfield (1990) demonstrated dose- and time-related changes in spontaneous EEGs of volunteers given 1.5, 3.0, or 6.0 mg of atropine in a balanced design. In this study, atropine increased delta power and decreased alpha power and reduced EEG indexes of vigilance, which were consistent with subjective reports of sleepiness and confusion. The effects at the low dose were only seen at 2 hr, whereas those at the highest dose lasted at least 8 hr.

The study by Ketchum et al. (1973) contained the most comprehensive account of atropine's effects on human cognitive function. They noted that the sequence of effects produced by high doses of the drug could be divided into three phases: induction, stupor, and delirium. In the induction phase, the peripherial autonomic effects were most conspicuous. This was overlapped by a second phase characterized by neurovegetative disturbances: somnolence, restlessness, incoordination, hyperthermia, and hyperreflexia. The third phase overlapped the second and was marked by disruption of awareness, attentional deficits, and inability to carry out instructions, to speak coherently, or to interpret stimuli correctly. The effects of a 6 mg per 70 kg of body weight (IM) dose of atropine are approximately equivalent to the ED_{50} doses (90–100 μg/kg) for affecting coordination, attention, and vision as determined in this study. The doses needed to produce disruptions in time estimation or produce hallucinations and partial amnesia are notably higher (130–160 μg/kg). However, it should be noted that these neurobehavioral effects were observed in young, healthy, well-rested volunteers under nonstressful conditions. Closer to a military scenario, Simmons et al. (1989) evaluated the effects of 2 mg and 4 mg of atropine (IM) on psychomotor and piloting performance in helicopter simulators. Likewise, Caldwell, Stephens, Carter, and Jones (1992) studied the effects of these same doses of atropine on helicopter pilot performance during actual flight conditions. Both studies concluded that the 2 mg dose of atropine would cause minimal performance impairment under most conditions, but the in-flight safety pilots did show some decrements. However, the 4 mg dose of atropine caused effects on vision, psychomotor performance, and cognitive skills such that flight performance was considered seriously impaired. A number of factors that may be common in combat or in some civilian settings may enhance the likelihood of observing some of these neurobehavioral effects at low (2 mg) doses. These factors include sleep deprivation, fatigue, mild dehydration, and thermal load from MOPP protective ensembles. For civilian populations, the additional factors of extreme youth or advanced age should be also be considered.

2-PAM Cl

The oxime 2-PAM Cl is administered to a nerve agent casualty to reactivate any "unaged" inhibited ChE. It is provided in autoinjectors in doses of 600 mg, and each military member is issued three autoinjectors (1,800 mg total dose) for immediate emergency treatment. A single IM autoinjector administration of 600 mg of 2-PAM Cl (8.9 mg/kg of body weight in a 70 kg-human) produces a maximal plasma concentration of 6.5 μg/ml (Sidell, 1974). This exceeds the 4 μg/ml concentration shown to reverse sarin-induced neuromuscular block in animals (Sundwall, 1961) and presumably will provide a therapeutic effect in man.

At the doses necessary to produce ChE reactivation, 2-PAM Cl does not produce side effects that would significantly impact performance. Calesnick, Christensen, and Richter (1967) studied the effects of oral, IM, or IV administered 2-PAM Cl within the dose range relevant to treatment of nerve agent casualties. With IM doses of 15 mg/kg there were no effects, whereas with IM doses of 30 mg/kg there were mild, transient elevations of systolic and diastolic blood pressure and an elevation of the T-wave in EKG tracings. These effects were considered to be of minimal clinical significance. Intravenous administration of 2-PAM Cl, however, produces more marked side effects. Dizziness and blurred vision were common complaints following IV doses of 5.0 to 7.5 mg/kg, but these symptoms subsided within 3 to 4 min; doses up to 10 mg/kg administered IM produced no cardiovascular or subjective symptoms in the same study (Sidell & Groff, 1971). A study cited in Headley (1982) reported no effects of a 600 mg IM dose of 2-PAM Cl on skin and rectal temperature or on sweat rate in a warm (104 °F) environment. When high doses of 2-PAM Cl are given orally either acutely (8 g) or repeatedly every 4 hrs (2–5 g) to achieve and maintain therapeutic blood levels for a 48-hr period, volunteers experienced diarrhea beginning 4 to 5 hr after a single high dose and from 10 to 30 hr after the first dose during the chronic dosing portion of the study (Sidell, Groff, & Ellin, 1969).

Diazepam

Diazepam is a benzodiazepine drug with anticonvulsant, antianxiety, sedative-hypnotic, and muscle-relaxant properties, and is available as an anticonvulsant treatment to prevent or stop nerve agent-induced seizures. Clinically, it is mostly used for its anticonvulsant and antianxiety properties because other benzodiazepine drugs have more specific sedative-hypnotic or muscle-relaxant effects. Military personnel are issued one 10-mg autoinjector of diazepam, which is to be administered by the casualty's fellow soldier or a medic at the onset of severe effects from a nerve agent (when the casualty's condition warrants the use of three MARK 1s at the same time), whether or not seizure activity is among the effects. Additional autoinjectors of diazepam are available to treat severely poisoned individuals by the combat medic who is authorized to give up to two more 10-mg injections of diazepam to convulsing casualties at 10-min intervals (*Medical Management of Chemical Casualties Handbook,* 1999).

Although it was once thought that diazepam had no addictive potential, experience has shown that its chronic use carries significant dependence liability and that withdrawal can be quite protracted (Ashton, 1994). Kleinknecht and Donaldson (1975) and Murray (1984) reviewed the effects of diazepam on cognitive and psychomotor performance. They concluded that, with the exception of simple reflex responding, diazepam impaired a number of different functions, including critical flicker fusion threshold, attention and vigilance, decision-making, learning and memory, and psychomotor performance. They also noted a strong interaction between the effects of diazepam and alcohol. Furthermore, an oral dose of 10 mg of diazepam produces a subjective sense of cognitive impairment and impairs auditory vigilance, resulting in a subjective rating correlating closely with the magnitude of the deficits (Roy-Byrne et al., 1987), and doses as low as 2.5 mg have been shown to impair vigilance (Koelega, 1989). Psychomotor performance on a variety of tasks is also affected for several hours following a dose of diazepam, and there is no evidence of tolerance development to this effect with repeated dosing (Smiley, 1987). It was also shown that oral doses of 0.1, 0.2, and 0.3 mg/kg diazepam produced dose- and time-dependent decreases in performance of immediate and delayed free recall of word lists (Ghoneim, Hinrichs, & Mewaldt, 1984), with the time to recover normal performance being 3.5, 4.5, and 5.5 hr, respectively. Based on this and other work (Gorissen, Curran, & Eling, 1998; Gorissen & Eling, 1998; Gorissen, Tielemans, & Coenen, 1997; Hinrichs, Mewaldt, Ghoneim, & Berie, 1982), it has been shown that the learning and memory deficit seen with diazepam is due to a specific impairment in the acquisition, not retrieval, of new information.

Pyridostigmine Bromide

PB is a peripherially acting carbamate drug that is used as a pretreatment when the threat of nerve agent attack is high. The rationale behind the development and use of PB has recently been presented by Dunn et al. (1997). Briefly, PB attaches (carbamolyation) to the same site on the AChE enzyme as the nerve agent, but the attachment of PB is only temporary. This carbamolyation of the AChE enzyme by PB prevents the binding of nerve agents and thus temporarily shields a fraction of the total AChE enzyme pool from irreversible inhibition by the nerve agent. Subsequent spontaneous decarbamolyation of the enzyme provides sufficient AChE to support vital functions, such as neuromuscular transmission to support respiration. PB pretreatment does not obviate the need for standard atropine/oxime therapy treatment after exposure, but it especially enhances the effectiveness of such treatment against agents that age rapidly (e.g., soman) or that are resistant to reactivation with 2-PAM (e.g., tabun, soman), or both. Pyridostigmine is available as 30-mg tablets to be taken every 8 hr, a regimen that is designed to produce inhibition of 20% to 40% of blood AChE. Because PB is a carbamate anticholinesterase, high doses of PB could produce peripherial signs of anticholinesterase intoxication—miosis, sweating, intestinal hypermotility, and salivation—that could degrade performance. Moreover, among all the medical countermeasures used by the military against nerve agent poisoning, PB is unique in that it is given chronically as a pretreatment to healthy individuals. Because of the varied and demanding requirements involved with most military-related jobs, the lack of adverse effects on performance was a key issue in the development of the concept of PB pretreatment. Both research and field experience have shown that, at the recommended dose and dosing schedule, PB produces minimal effects that would impact performance.

Gall (1981) summarized British studies of PB, which found no changes in memory, manual dexterity, vigilance, day or night driving ability, or tests of cognitive and motor skills. Kay and Morrison (1988) found a small increase in contrast sensitivity due to a small reduction in pupil diameter and concluded that PB would have no deleterious effects on stationary visual function. Various aspects of pilot performance have been assessed in several studies, and significant effects of PB have been found on flight simulator performance (Izraeli et al., 1990) or on in-flight air crew performance (Gawron, Schiflett, Miller, Slater, & Ball, 1990). Likewise, there were no effects on cognitive function or pilot performance as a result of PB administration under conditions of altitude (Schiflett, Stranges, Slater, & Jackson, 1987) or acceleration tolerance (Forster et al., 1994). Kolka and colleagues (Cook, Kolka, & Wenger, 1992; Kolka & Stephenson, 1990; Stephenson & Kolka, 1990; Wenger, Quigley, & Kolka, 1993) studied the effects of PB administration on endurance and exercise physiology under a variety of environmental conditions and found only modest decreases in heart rate and skin blood flow that had no adverse effect on the ability to perform work. In another study, Keeler, Hurst, and Dunn (1991) performed a retrospective analysis of physiological changes produced by PB in over 40,000 soldiers who took the drug during the 1991 Persian Gulf War. About half the soldiers reported physiological changes, which included increased flatus, abdominal cramps, soft stools, and urinary urgency. Fewer than 0.1% of the soldiers exhibited any symptoms severe enough to warrant discontinuation of the drug. A similar report from the Israeli Defence Force (Sharabi et al., 1991) noted that symptoms of chronic PB administration were infrequent and mild. When symptoms did occur, they started approximately 1.6 hr after each dose, and there was no relation between type or severity of symptom and level of cholinesterase inhibition.

Although the effects of PB on performance appear to be negligible under most circumstances, there is some evidence that asthma may be exacerbated by this drug (Keeler et al., 1991). Gouge, Daniels, and Smith (1994) studied a group of asthmatic soldiers who participated in the 1991 Persian Gulf War and found no changes in forced vital capacity following PB but did see a worsening of asthmatic symptoms in 7 of the 10 asthmatics studied. The severity of the exacerbation correlated with the severity of asthma symptoms experienced by the soldiers in the desert and inversely with body weight. They proposed that the irritant effect of the dust in the desert may have predisposed the condition of asthmatics to worsen after PB. Another factor noted by both Keeler et al. (1991) and Gouge et al. (1994) was that adverse side effects of PB were more likely to be observed in individuals of low body weight because they would receive a higher dose on a weight (mg/kg) basis. In addition, because PB is taken as a prophylaxis, the possibility of adverse interactions with other commonly used military medications was evaluated by Keeler (1990). However, she found no pharmacological basis for potential adverse interactions between PB and commonly used antibiotics, anesthetics, or analgesics but did note that there was a possibility for an interaction with muscle relaxants used during anesthesia induction.

CONCLUSIONS

Exposure to nerve agents produces immediate and long-term effects on neurobehavioral function and performance that are dependent on the route and severity of exposure. The more severe the initial exposure, the greater the intensity and duration of the immediate toxic effects and the time for recovery of normal function. It needs to be stressed that the return to "normal" may take many weeks or months following severe exposures and that even mild to moderate exposures may compromise functions for days or weeks. Administration of medical countermeasures may relieve some of the life-threatening toxic signs of poisoning but will not totally reverse all toxic effects that compromise performance. This is certainly the case where exposure produces severe toxic effects. The protracted time for full recovery following moderate to severe exposures and the possibility of subclinical long-term effects following severe exposures are probably the two features of nerve-agent poisoning that are not widely recognized.

Most of the compounds that are used as medical countermeasures for nerve-agent exposure can be expected to have minimal or at least self-limiting effects on performance if used in accordance with training and doctrine. PB pretreatment proved to have minimal negative impacts on military performance when used during the 1991 Persian Gulf War. It should be noted, however, that under those circumstances, soldiers with a wide range of duties, performance demands, and additional stressors successfully used PB without any operationally significant impairment in combat effectiveness.

The medical countermeasure emergency treatment compounds (atropine, 2-PAM Cl, and diazepam) would only impact performance if they were taken as a false alarm in the absence of a true exposure or when the level of exposure was so low as to not warrant their use. Soldiers are trained only to self-administer a single MARK 1 kit if mild to moderate signs or symptoms of nerve-agent poisoning occur following a vapor exposure, or up to two MARK 1 kits (depending on severity of symptoms) if the exposure was to a liquid nerve agent. It is assumed that a causality who experiences signs or symptoms requiring more extensive treatment will be unable to self-administer aid and that this will be provided by a fellow soldier or a medic. Performance effects from inadvertent administration of the MARK 1 kit would be almost entirely from the atropine. The 2-mg dose of atropine in a single MARK 1 was chosen because it reverses the effects of moderate doses of nerve agents; individuals can tolerate the associated side effects of a dose this size while maintaining reasonably normal performance. It is a compromise between the dose that is therapeutically desirable and the dose that can be safely administered to a nonintoxicated individual. The inadvertent administration of all three MARK 1 kits, or the diazepam autoinjector, or both, even under the stress of battlefield conditions, would have to be considered a highly unlikely event. In the event an individual did inject all the treatment drugs available to them under the false impression they had been exposed to nerve agent, the most pronounced and prolonged effects on neurobehavioral function and performance would be produced by the 6 mg of atropine. Performance on specific tasks could be significantly degraded anywhere from 8 hr (vigilance, coordination, and cognitive tasks) to over 24 hr (dilated pupils). Thorough training in recognizing the signs and symptoms of nerve-agent exposure and the appropriate use of the MARK 1 kits is the best strategy to prevent this potential problem.

ACKNOWLEDGMENTS

The opinions or assertions contained herein are the private views of the author and are not to be construed as reflecting the views of the Department of the Army or the Department of Defense.

REFERENCES

Ames, R., Steenland, K., Jenkins, B., Chrislop, D., & Russo, J. (1995). Chronic neurological sequelae to cholinesterase inhibition among agricultural pesticide applicators. *Archives of Environmental Health, 50,* 440–443.

Ashton, H. (1994). The treatment of benzodiazepine dependence. *Addiction, 89,* 1535–1541.

Baghdoyan, H. A., Monaco, A. P., Rodrigo-Angulo, M. L., Assens, F., McCarley, R. W., & Hobson, J. A. (1984). Microinjections of neostigmine into the pontine reticular formation of cats enhances desynchronized sleep signs. *Journal of Pharmacology and Experimental Therapeutics, 231,* 173–180.

Baker, R., Adams, A., Jampolsky, A., Brown, B., Haegerstrom-Portnoy, G., & Jones, R. (1983). Effects of atropine on visual performance. *Military Medicine, 148,* 530–535 .

Bartus, R. T., Dean, R. L., Beer, B., & Lippa, A. S. (1982). The cholinergic hypothesis of geriatric memory dysfunction. *Science, 217,* 408–417.

Bowers, M. B., Goodman, E., & Sim, V. M. (1964). Some behavioral changes in man following anticholinesterase administration. *Journal of Nervous and Mental Disorders, 138,* 383–389.

Brimblecombe, R. W. (1974). Drug action on cholinergic systems. Baltimore: University Park Press.

Burchfiel, J. L., Duffy, F. H., & Sim, V. M. (1976). Persistent effects of sarin and dieldrin upon the primate electroencephalogram. *Toxicology and Applied Pharmacology, 35,* 365–379.

Caldwell, J. A., Stephens, R. L., Carter, D. J., & Jones, H. D. (1992). Effects of 2 mg and 4 mg atropine sulfate on the performance of U.S. Army helicopter pilots. *Aviation, Space, and Environmental Medicine, 63,* 857–864.

Calesnick, B., Christensen, J. A., & Richter, M. (1967). Human toxicity of various oximes. *Archives of Environmental Health, 15,* 599–608.

Cook, J. E., Kolka, M. A., & Wenger, C. B. (1992). Chronic pyridostigmine bromide administration: Side effects among soldiers working in a desert environment. *Military Medicine, 157,* 250–254.

Craig, A. B., & Freeman, G. (1953). *Clinical observations in workers accidentally exposed to "G"-agents* (Medical Laboratory Res. Rep. No. 154). Aberdeen Proving Ground, MD: Edgewood Arsenal.

Davis, K. L., Berger, P. A., Hollister, L. E., & Barchas, J. D. (1978). Cholinergic involvement in mental disorders. *Life Sciences, 22,* 1865–1871.

Dawson, R. M. (1994). Review of oximes available for treatment of nerve agent poisoning. *Journal of Applied Toxicology, 14,* 317–331.

DeCandole, C. A., Douglas, W. W., Evans, C. L., Holmes, R., Spencer, K. E. V., Torrance, R. W., et al. (1953). The failure of respiration in death by anticholinesterase poisoning. *British Journal of Pharmacology, 8,* 466–475.

Duffy, F. H., Burchfiel, J. L., Bartels, P. H., Gaon, M., & Sim, V. M. (1979). Long-term effects of an organophosphate upon the human encephalogram. *Toxicology and Applied Pharmacology, 47,* 161–176.

Dunn, M. A., Hackley, B. E., Jr., & Sidell, F. R. (1997). Pretreatment for nerve agent exposure. In R. Zajtchuk (Ed.), *Textbook of military medicine: Medical aspects of chemical and biological warfare* (pp. 181–196). Washington, DC: Office of the Surgeon General.

Forster, E. M., Barber, J. A., Parker, F. R., Jr., Whinnery, J. E., Burton, R. R., & Boll, P. (1994). Effect of pyridostigmine bromide on acceleration tolerance and performance. *Aviation, Space, and Environmental Medicine, 65,* 110–116.

Gall, D. (1981). The use of therapeutic mixtures in the treatment of cholinesterase inhibition. *Fundamental and Applied Pharmacology, 1,* 214–216.

Gawron, V. J., Schiflett, S. G., Miller, J. C., Slater, T., & Ball, J. F. (1990). Effects of pyridostigmine bromide on in-flight aircrew performance. *Human Factors, 32,* 79–94.

George, R., Haslett, W. L., & Jenden, D. J. (1964). A cholinergic mechanism in the brainstem reticular formation: Induction of paradoxical sleep. *International Journal of Neuropharmacology, 3,* 541–552.

Ghoneim, M. M., Hinrichs, J. V., & Mewaldt, M. P. (1984). Dose-response analysis of the behavioral effects of diazepam: I. Learning and memory. *Psychopharmacology, 82,* 291–295.

Gillin, J. C., Sitram, N., Mendelson, W. B., & Wyatt, R. J. (1978). Physostigmine alters onset but not duration of REM sleep in man. *Psychopharmacology, 58,* 111–114.

Glenn, J. F., Hinman, D. J., & McMaster, S. B. (1987). Electroencephalographic correlates of nerve agent poisoning. In N. J. Dun & R. L. Perlman (Eds.), *Neurobiology of acetylcholine* (pp. 503–534). New York: Plenum.

Gnadt, J. W., Atwood, C. W., Meighen, G. A., & Pegram, G. V. (1986). Di-isopropyl-fluorophosphate (DFP): Acute toxicity and sleep. *Neurotoxicology, 7,* 165–172.

Gnadt, J. W., & Pegram, G. V. (1986). Cholinergic brainstem mechanisms of REM sleep in the rat. *Brain Research, 384,* 29–41.

Gnadt, J. W., Pegram, G. V., & Baxter, J. F. (1985). The acetylcholinesterase inhibitor di-isopropyl-fluorophosphate increases REM sleep in rats. *Physiology and Behavior, 35,* 911–916.

Gorissen, M. E., Curran, H. V., & Eling, P. A. (1998). Proactive interference and temporal context encoding after diazepam intake. *Psychopharmacology, 138,* 334–343.

Gorissen, M. E., & Eling, P. A. (1998). Dual task performance after diazepam intake: Can resource depletion explain the benzodiazepine-induced amnesia? *Psychopharmacology, 138,* 354–361.

Gorissen, M. E., Tielemans, M., & Coenen, A. (1997). Alertness and memory after sleep deprivation and diazepam intake. *Journal of Psychopharmacology, 11,* 233–239.

Gouge, S. F., Daniels, D. J., & Smith, C. E. (1994). Exacerbation of asthma after pyridostigmine during Operation Desert Storm. *Military Medicine, 159,* 108–111.

Grob, D., & Harvey, A. M. (1953). The effects and treatment of nerve gas poisoning. *American Journal of Medicine, 14,* 52–63.

Grob, D., & Harvey, A. M. (1958). Effects in man of the anticholinesterase compound sarin (isopropyl methyl phosphonofluoridate). *Journal of Clinical Investigations, 37,* 350–368.

Grob, D., Harvey, A. M., Langworthy, O. R., & Lilenthal, J. L. (1947). The administration of di-isopropyl flurophosphate (DFP) to man: III. Effect on the central nervous system with special reference to the electrical activity of the brain. *Bulletin of the Johns Hopkins Hospital, 81,* 257–266.

Haegerstrom-Portnoy, G., Jones, R., Adams, A., & Jampolsky, A. (1987). Effects of atropine and 2-PAM Cl on vision and performance in humans. *Aviation, Space, and Environmental Medicine, 58,* 47–53.

Hatta, K., Miura, Y., Asukai, N., & Hamabe, Y. (1996). Amnesia from sarin poisoning. *Lancet, 347,* 1343.

Hayes, W. (1982). *Pesticides studied in man.* Baltimore: Williams & Wilkins.

Headley, D. B. (1982). Effects of atropine sulfate and pralidoxime chloride on visual, physiological, performance, subjective, and cognitive variables in man: A review. *Military Medicine, 147,* 122–132.

Higgins, S. T., Woodward, B. M., & Henningfield, J. E. (1989). Effects of atropine on the repeated acquisition and performance of response sequences in humans. *Journal for the Experimental Analysis of Behavior, 51,* 5–15.

Hinrichs, J. V., Mewaldt, S. P., Ghoneim, M. M., & Berie, J. L. (1982). Diazepam and learning: Assessment of acquisition deficits. *Pharmacology Biochemistry and Behavior, 17,* 165–170.

Hobson, J. A. (1992). Sleep and dreaming: Induction and mediation of REM sleep by cholinergic mechanisms. *Current Opinions in Neurobiology, 2,* 759–763.

Holmes, J. H., & Gaon, M. D. (1956). Observations on acute and multiple exposure to anticholinesterase agents. *Transactions of the American Clinical and Climatology Society, 68,* 86–101.

Izraeli, S., Avgar, D., Almog, S., Shochat, I., Tochner, Z., Tamir, A., et al. (1990). The effect of repeated doses of 30 mg pyridostigmine bromide on pilot performance in an A-4 flight simulator. *Aviation, Space, and Environmental Medicine, 61,* 430–432.

Janowsky, D. S., & Overstreet, D. H. (1990). Cholinergic dysfunction in depression. *Pharmacology and Toxicology, 66,* 100–111.

Janowsky, D. S., Risch, S. C., & Gillin, J. C. (1983). Adrenergic-cholinergic balance and the treatment of affective disorders. *Progress in Neuropsychopharmacology and Biological Psychiatry, 7,* 297–307.

Kato, T., & Hamanaka, T. (1996). Ocular signs and symptoms caused by exposure to sarin gas. *American Journal of Ophthalmology, 121,* 209–210.

Kay, C. D., & Morrison, J. D. (1988). The effects of ingestion of 60 mg pyridostigmine bromide on contrast sensitivity in man. *Human Toxicology, 7,* 347–352.

Keeler, J. R. (1990). Interactions between nerve agent pretreatment and drugs commonly used in combat anesthesia. *Military Medicine, 155,* 527–533.

Keeler, J. R., Hurst, C. G., & Dunn, M. A. (1991). Pyridostigmine used as a nerve agent pretreatment under war time conditions. *Journal of the American Medical Association, 266,* 693–695.

Ketchum, J. S., Sidell, F. R., Crowell, E. B., Jr., Aghajanian, G. K., & Hayes, A. H., Jr. (1973). Atropine, scopolamine, and ditran: Comparative pharmacology and antagonists in man. *Psychopharmacologia, 28,* 121–145.

Kleinknecht, R. A., & Donaldson, D. (1975). A review of the effects of diazepam on cognitive and pyschomotor performance. *Journal of Nervous and Mental Disorders, 161,* 399–414.

Kobrick, J. L., Johnson, R. F., & McMenemy, D. J. (1990). Effects of nerve agent antidote and heat exposure on soldier performance in the BDU and MOPP-IV ensembles. *Military Medicine, 155,* 159–162.

Koelega, H. S. (1989). Benzodiazepines and vigilance performance: A review. *Psychopharmacology, 98,* 145–156.

Koelle, G. B. (1963). Cholinesterases and anticholinesterase agents. In O. Eichler & A. Farah (Eds.), *Handbuch der Experimentellen Pharmakologie* (Vol. 15). Berlin, Germany: Springer-Verlag.

Kolka, M. A., & Stephenson, L. A. (1990). Human temperature regulation during exercise after oral pyridostigmine administration. *Aviation, Space, and Environmental Medicine, 61,* 220–224.

Korsak, R. J., & Sato, M. M. (1977). Effects of chronic organophosphate pesticide exposure on the central nervous system. *Clinical Toxicology, 11,* 83–95.

Krueger, G. P., & Banderet, L. E. (1997). Effects of chemical protective clothing on military performance: A review of the issues. *Military Psychology, 9,* 255–286.

Longo, V. G. (1966). Behavioral and electroencephalographic effects of atropine and related compounds. *Pharmacological Reviews, 18,* 965–996.

Masuda, N., Takatsu, M., Morinari, H., & Ozawa, T. (1995). Sarin poisoning in Tokyo subway. *Lancet, 345,* 1446.

McDonough, J. H., & Shih, T. M. (1997). Neuropharmacological mechanisms of nerve agent-induced seizure and neuropathology. *Neuroscience and Biobehavioral Reviews, 21,* 559–579.

Medical management of chemical casualties handbook (3rd ed.). (1999). Aberdeen Proving Ground, MD: U.S. Army Medical Research Institute of Chemical Defense, Chemical Casualty Care Office.

Metcalf, D. R., & Holmes, J. W. (1969). EEG, psychological, and neurological alterations in humans with organophosphorus exposure. *Annals of the New York Academy of Science, 160,* 357–365.

Mewaldt, S. P., & Ghoneim, M. M. (1979). The effects and interactions of scopolamine, physostigmine and methamphetamine on human memory. *Pharmacology Biochemistry and Behavior, 10,* 205–210.

Moore, D. H., Clifford, C. B., Crawford, I. T., Cole, G. M., & Baggett, J. M. (1995). Review of nerve agent inhibitors and reactivators of acetylcholinesterase. In D. M. Quinn, A. S. Balasubramanian, B. P. Doctor, & P. Taylor (Eds.), *Enzymes of cholinesterase family* (pp. 297–304). New York: Plenum.

Morita, H., Yanaagisawa, N., Nakajima, T., Shimizu, M., Hirabayashi, H., Okudera, H., et al. (1995). Sarin poisoning in Masumoto, Japan. *Lancet, 346,* 290–293.

Moylan-Jones, R. J. (1969). The effect of a large dose of atropine on the performance of routine tasks. *British Journal of Pharmacology, 37,* 301–305.

Moylan-Jones, R. J., & Thomas, D. P. (1973). Cyclopentolate in treatment of sarin miosis. *British Journal of Pharmacology, 48,* 309–313.

Murray, J. T. (1984). Effects of valium and librium on human psychomotor and cognitive functions. *Genetic Psychology Monographs, 109,* 167–197.

Nakajima, T., Ohta, S., Morita, H., Midorikawa, Y., Mimura, S., & Yanagisawa, N. (1997). Epidemiological study of sarin poisoning in Matsumoto City, Japan. *Journal of Epidemiology, 8,* 33–41.

National Research Council. (1982). *Possible long-term health effects of short-term exposure to chemical agents: Vol. 1. Anticholinesterases and anticholinergics.* Washington, DC: National Academy Press.

Nozaki, H., & Aikawa, N. (1995). Sarin poisoning in Tokyo subway. *Lancet, 345,* 1446–1447.

Nozaki, H., Aikawa, N., Fujishima, S., Suzuki, M., Shinozawa, Y., Hori, S., et al. (1995). A case of VX poisoning and the difference from sarin. *Lancet, 346,* 698–699.

Ohbu, S., Yamashina, A., Takasu, N., Yamaguchi, T., Murai, T., Nakano, K., et al. (1997). Sarin poisoning on Tokyo subway. *Southern Medical Journal, 90,* 587–593.

Okumura, T., Takasu, N., Ishimatsu, S., Miyanoki, S., Mitsuhashi, A., Kumada, K., et al. (1996). Report on 640 victims of the Tokyo subway sarin attack. *Annals of Emergency Medicine, 28,* 129–135.

Penetar, D. M. (1990). A brief review of atropine effects on physiology and performance. *Drug Development Research, 20,* 117–121.

Penetar, D. M., & Beatrice, E. S. (1986). Effects of atropine on human pursuit tracking performances. *Aviation, Space, and Environmental Medicine, 57,* 654–658.

Penetar, D. M., Haegerstrom-Portnoy, G., & Jones, R. T. (1988). Combined atropine and 2-PAM Cl effects on tracking performance and visual, physiological, and psychological functions. *Aviation, Space, and Environmental Medicine, 59,* 1125–1132.

Penetar, D. M., & McDonough, J. H. (1983). Effects of cholinergic drugs on delayed match-to-sample performance of rhesus monkeys. *Pharmacology Biochemistry and Behavior, 19,* 963–967.

Pickworth, W. B., Herning, R. I., Koeppl, B., & Henningfield, J. E. (1990). Dose-dependent atropine-induced changes in spontaneous electroencephalogram in human volunteers. *Military Medicine, 155,* 166–170.

Rengstorff, R. H. (1985). Accidental exposure to sarin. *Archives of Toxicology, 56,* 201–203.

Rickett, D. L., Glenn, J. F., & Beers, E. T. (1986). Central respiratory effects versus neuromuscular actions of nerve agents. *Neurotoxicology, 7,* 225–236.

Rosenstock, L., Keifer, M., Daniell, W. E., McConnell, R., & Claypoole, K. (1991). Chronic central nervous system effects of acute organophosphate pesticide intoxication. *Lancet, 338,* 223–227.

Roy-Byrne, P. P., Uhde, T. W., Holcomb, H., Thompson, K., King, A. K., & Weingartner, H. (1987). The effects of diazepam on cognitive process in normal subjects. *Psychopharmacology, 91,* 30–33.

Rubin, L. S., & Goldberg, M. N. (1958). Effect of tertiary and quaternary atropine salts on absolute scotopic threshold changes produced by an anticholinesterase (sarin). *Journal of Applied Physiology, 12,* 302–310.

Rubin, L. S., Krop, S., & Goldberg, M. N. (1957). Effect of sarin on dark adaptation in man. *Journal of Applied Physiology, 11,* 445–449.

Savage, E. P., Keefe, T. J., Mounce, L. M., Heaton, R. K., Lewis, J. A., & Burcar, P. J. (1988). Chronic neurological sequelae of acute organophosphate pesticide poisoning. *Archives of Environmental Health, 43,* 38–45.

Schiflett, S. G., Stranges, S. F., Slater, T., & Jackson, M. K. (1987). Interactive effects of pyridostigmine and altitude on performance. In *Proceedings of the 6th Medical Chemical Defense Bioscience Review* (pp. 605–607). Aberdeen Proving Ground, MD: U.S. Army Medical Research Institute of Chemical Defense. (DTIC No. AD–B121 516)

Sekijima, Y., Morita, H., Shindo, M., Okudera, H., Shibata, T., & Yanagisawa, N. (1995). A case of severe sarin poisoning in the sarin attack at Matsumoto—One-year follow-up on the clinical findings and laboratory data. *Rinsho Shinkeijaku, 35,* 1241–1245.

Sharabi, Y., Danon, Y. L., Berkenstadt, H., Almog, S., Mimouni-Bloch, A., Zisman, A., et al. (1991). Survey of symptoms following intake of pyridostigmine during the Persian Gulf war. *Israel Journal of Medical Science, 27,* 656–658.

Shih, T. M., Koviak, T. A., & Capacio, B. R. (1991). Anticonvulsants for poisoning by the organophosphorus compound soman: Pharmacological mechanisms. *Neuroscience and Biobehavioral Reviews, 15,* 349–362.

Shih, T. M., & McDonough, J. H. (1997). Neurochemical mechanisms in soman-induced seizures. *Journal of Applied Toxicology, 17,* 255–264.

Shih, T. M., McDonough, J. H., & Koplovitz, I. (1999). Anticonvulsants for soman-induced seizure activity. *Journal of Biomedical Science, 6,* 86–96.

Sidell, F. R. (1974). Soman and sarin: Clinical manifestations and treatment of accidental poisoning by organophosphates. *Clinical Toxicology, 7,* 1–17.

Sidell, F. R. (1992). Clinical considerations in nerve agent intoxication. In S. Somani (Ed.), *Chemical warfare agents* (pp. 155–194). New York: Academic.

Sidell, F. R. (1996). A history of human studies with nerve agents by the UK and USA. In T. C. Marrs, R. L. Maynard, & F. R. Sidell (Eds.), *Chemical warfare agents: Toxicology and treatment* (pp. 115–137). Chichester, England: Wiley.

Sidell, F. R. (1997). Nerve agents. In R. Zajtchuk (Ed.), *Textbook of military medicine: Medical aspects of chemical and biological warfare* (pp. 129–179). Washington, DC: Office of the Surgeon General.

Sidell, F. R., & Groff, W. A. (1971). Intramuscular and intravenous administrations of small doses of 2-pyridinium aldoxime methochloride to man. *Journal of Pharmaceutical Science, 60,* 1224–1228.

Sidell, F. R., Groff, W. A., & Ellin, R. I. (1969). Blood levels of oxime and symptoms in humans after single and multiple oral doses of 2-pyridine aldoxime methochloride. *Journal of Pharmaceutical Science, 58,* 1093–1098.

Simmons, R. R., Caldwell, J. A., Stephens, R. L., Stone, L. W., Carter, D. J., Behar, I., et al. (1989). *Effects of the chemical defense antidote atropine sulfate on helicopter pilot performance: A simulator study* (USAARL Tech. Rep. No. 89–17). Fort Rucker, AL: U.S. Army Aeromedical Research Laboratory.

Sitram, N., Wyatt, R. J., Dawson, S., & Gillin, J. G. (1976). REM sleep induction by physostigmine infusion during sleep. *Science, 191,* 1281–1283.

Smiley, A. (1987). Effects of minor tranquilizers and antidepressants on psychomotor performance. *Journal of Clinical Psychiatry, 48,* 22–28.

Somani, S. M., Solana, R. P., & Dube, S. N. (1992). Toxicodynamics of nerve agents. In S. Somani (Ed.), *Chemical warfare agents* (pp. 68–123). New York: Academic.

Stephens, R., Spurgeon, A., Calvert, I. A., Beach, J., Levy, L. S., Berry, H., et al. (1995). Neuropsychological effects of long-term exposure to organophosphates in sheep dip. *Lancet, 345,* 1135–1139.

Stephenson, L. A., & Kolka, M. A. (1990). Acetylcholinesterase inhibitor, pyridostigmine bromide, reduces skin blood flow in humans. *American Journal of Physiology, 258,* R951–R957.

Stewart, W. C., Madill, H. D., & Dyer, A. M. (1968). Night vision in the miotic eye. *Canadian Medical Association Journal, 99,* 1145–1148.

Stokes, L., Stark, A., Marshall, E., & Narang, A. (1995). Neurotoxicity among pesticide applicators exposed to organophosphates. *Occupational and Environmental Medicine, 52,* 648–653.

Sundwall, A. (1961). Minimum concentrations of n-methylpyridinium-2-aldoxime methan sulphonate (P2S) which reverse neuromuscular block. *Biochemical Pharmacology, 8,* 413–417.

Taylor, P. (1985). Anticholinesterase agents. In A. G. Gilman, L. S. Goodman, T. W. Rall, & F. Murad (Eds.), *The pharmacological basis of therapeutics* (6th ed., pp. 110–129). New York: Macmillan.

Voytko, M. L. (1996). Cognitive functions of the basal forebrain cholinergic system in monkeys: Memory or attention? *Behavioral Brain Research, 75,* 13–25.

Wenger, B., Quigley, M. D., & Kolka, M. A. (1993). Seven-day pyridostigmine administration and thermoregulation during rest and exercise in dry heat. *Aviation, Space, and Environmental Medicine, 64,* 905–911.

Wetherell, A. (1980). Some effects of atropine on short-term memory. *British Journal of Clinical Pharmacology, 10,* 627–628.

Wright, P. G. (1954). An analysis of the central and peripheral components of respiratory failure produced by anticholinesterase poisoning in the rabbit. *Journal of Physiology, 126,* 52–70.

Yokoyama, K., Araki, S., Murata, K., Nishikitani, M., Okumura, T., Ishimatsu, S., et al. (1998a). Chronic neurobehavioral and central and autonomic nervous system effects of Tokyo subway sarin poisoning. *Journal of Physiology (Paris), 92,* 317–323.

Yokoyama, K., Araki, S., Murata, K., Nishikitani, M., Okumura, T., Ishimatsu, S., et al. (1998b). A preliminary study on delayed vestibulo-cerebellar effects of Tokyo subway sarin poisoning in relation to gender difference: Frequency analysis of postural sway. *Journal of Occupational and Environmental Medicine, 40,* 17–21.

MILITARY PSYCHOLOGY, 2002, *14*(2), 121–143

Nerve Agent Bioscavengers: Protection With Reduced Behavioral Effects

Douglas M. Cerasoli and David E. Lenz
Biochemical Pharmacology Branch
U.S. Army Medical Research Institute of Chemical Defense
Aberdeen Proving Ground, Maryland

Although treatments for intoxication by organophosphorus nerve agents exist, the treatment regimens suffer from undesirable side effects. To overcome these disadvantages, the use of bioscavengers has emerged as a new approach to reduce the in vivo toxicity of chemical warfare nerve agents. Bioscavengers fall into two broad categories: stoichiometric (i.e., proteins that bind a poison in some fixed ratio) and catalytic (i.e., proteins that can cause the breakdown of a molecule of a poison, regenerate, and then repeat the process until all of the poison molecules have been destroyed). To be an improvement of current treatments, a biological scavenger should have no or minimal behavioral or physiological side effects, should provide protection against one or more nerve agents up to 5 times the median lethal dose (5 LD_{50}), and should reduce or eliminate any behavioral or physiological side effects normally associated with the currently fielded therapy. Studies with equine or human butyrylcholinesterase or fetal bovine serum acetylcholinesterase show that none of these scavengers exhibit behavioral side effects when administered to rats or monkeys. These three scavengers as well as carboxylesterase are each capable of providing protection against 2 to 16 LD_{50}s of GD, GB, or VX depending on the scavenger and the test species (rat, mouse, rabbit, guinea pig, or rhesus monkey). When behavioral testing was performed on animals pretreated with a bioscavenger and then administered up to 5 LD_{50}s of GD or VX, either no, or only very minor, transient deficits were reported. These results are in stark contrast to the prolonged (1 to 2 week) behavioral incapacitation experienced by animals pretreated with pyridostigmine and then exposed to the same dose of nerve agent followed by the standard atropine, oxime

This article is part of a special issue, "Chemical Warfare and Chemical Terrorism: Psychological and Performance Outcomes," of *Military Psychology*, 2002, *14*(2), 83–177.

Requests for reprints should be sent to David E. Lenz, Biochemical Pharmacology Branch, U.S. Army Medical Research Institute of Chemical Defense, 3100 Ricketts Point Road, Aberdeen Proving Ground, MD 21010–5400.

therapy with or without diazepam. Although several challenges still remain before bioscavengers could augment or replace the current therapeutic regimes for nerve agent intoxication, the results to date offer impressive evidence for the value of this approach as the next generation of pharmaceuticals to afford protection against nerve agent poisoning with a virtual absence of behavioral side effects.

Organophosphorus compounds, usually esters, amides, or thiol derivatives of phosphoric acid, are among the most toxic substances identified (Dacre, 1984). Originally, organophosphorus compounds were developed for use as insecticides (Ballantyne & Marrs, 1992), but their extreme toxicity toward higher vertebrates has led to their adoption as weapons of warfare (Maynard & Beswick, 1992). The organophosphorus compounds most commonly used as chemical weapons (referred to as nerve agents) are tabun (GA), sarin (GB), soman (GD), cyclohexylmethyl phosphonofluoridate (GF), and ethyl-S-diisopropylaminoethyl methylphosphonothiolate (VX). The nerve agents are small compounds of low molecular weight (ranging from 140 to 267 atomic mass units) and under standard conditions are all liquids that differ in their degrees of volatility (Somani, Solana, & Dube, 1992). They have median lethal dose (LD_{50}) values in mammals, including estimates for humans, in the μg/kg dose range for all routes of exposure except dermal, where LD_{50} doses are in the mg/kg range (Maynard & Beswick, 1992).

Organophosphorus compounds produce their toxic effects by irreversibly inhibiting the enzyme acetylcholinesterase (Koelle, 1963; Taylor, 1990), which leads to an increase in the concentration of acetylcholine in the cholinergic synapses of both the peripheral and central nervous systems (CNS). The physiological consequences of elevated acetylcholine include alterations in the function of the respiratory center (Brimblecombe, 1977; de Candole et al., 1953; Stewart, 1959; Stewart & Anderson, 1968) and overstimulation at neuromuscular junctions (Bajgar, Jakl, & Hrdina, 1971; Chabrier & Jacob, 1980; Heffron & Hobbinger, 1979). A sufficiently high level of acetylcholine or a sufficiently rapid increase in acetylcholine concentration precipitates a cholinergic crisis that can result in dimming of vision, headache, shortness of breath, muscle weakness, seizures, or a combination of all of these symptoms. In the extreme, organophosphorus intoxication can be life threatening, with death usually resulting from respiratory failure. This is often accompanied by secondary cardiovascular components, including hypotension, cardiac slowing, and arrhythmias (Taylor, 1990).

CURRENT THERAPY FOR NERVE AGENT EXPOSURE

The conventional approach to treatment of organophosphorus intoxication involves efforts to counteract the effects of AChE inhibition. The administration of cholinolytic drugs such as atropine, which function by blocking acetylcholine receptors, antagonizes the effects of elevated acetylcholine levels that result from the inhibition of AChE (Heath & Meredith, 1992). In addition, an oxime is given that reacts with the inhibited (phosphonylated) AChE to displace the phosphoryl group and restore normal activity (Wilson & Ginsburg, 1955). In the United States, the oxime of choice for treatment of nerve agent poisoning is the chloride salt of 2-PAM, usually referred to as 2-PAM Cl, although bis-pyridinium oximes may be more effective depending on the particular organophosphorus agent (Bismuth, Inns, & Marrs, 1992). Anticonvulsant drugs such as diazepam are also administered to control organophosphorus-induced tremors and convulsions. Finally, individuals at high risk for exposure to nerve agents are pretreated with an easily reversible AChE inhibitor such as pyridostigmine, which partially and temporarily masks the active site of AChE and thus protects the enzyme from irreversible inhibition by the organophosphorus agent (Gordon, Leadbeater, & Maidment, 1978). A more thorough review of the state of current therapeutic approaches for nerve agent poisoning can be found in the article by McDonough (2002/this issue).

Although these treatment regimens have been standard for many years, they are not ideal and suffer from a number of disadvantages. The major drawback of current approaches is that, although they can be effective in preventing lethality, they do not prevent performance deficits, behavioral incapacitation, loss of consciousness, or permanent brain damage, all of which can result from acute organophosphorus toxicity (Leadbeater, Inns, & Rylands, 1985). In addition, these treatments can produce serious side effects if administered in the absence of any cholinesterase inhibitors. For example, cholinolytics such as atropine, which are acetylcholine antagonists, given in the absence of a cholinergic crisis, can cause impairment of CNS function due to the blockade of muscarinic receptors (McDonough & Penetar, 1982; Wenger, 1979). It is worth noting that the overt manifestations that could result following administration of excess atropine include disorientation, memory impairment, agitation, and predominantly visual, but also tactile and olfactory, hallucinations and illusions. Oximes have been reported to produce transient dizziness, headache, and increases in blood pressure and heart rate (Erdmann, Bosse, & Franke, 1965; Sidell & Groff, 1970; Vojvodic, 1970; Wiezorek, Kreisel, Schnitzlein, & Matzkowski, 1968), as well as antinicotinic and antimuscarinic effects (Clement, 1982). Pyridostigmine is a potent cholinesterase inhibitor in its own right, although it spontaneously decarbamylates fairly rapidly (half-life of approximately 3 hr; Reiner, 1971); the side effects of this pretreatment compound have been well documented (Dunn & Sidell, 1989; Huff, 1986). In addition to their undesirable physiologic side effects, achievement of maximum effectiveness by conventional nerve agent antidotes requires their administration within a fairly prescribed time frame with respect to nerve agent exposure (Dunn & Sidell, 1989) due to the rapid action of organophosphorus agents once they enter the bloodstream. Prompt postexposure administration of antidotes can be facilitated by the use of autoinjectors (Dunn & Sidell, 1989) but still represents a substantial logistical challenge to either civilians or soldiers in the field.

Several nerve agents, including GF, sarin, and particularly soman, present an additional therapeutic challenge in that, after they inhibit AChE, they undergo a second reaction in which the inhibited enzyme is dealkylated. The result is an inhibited form of AChE that is resistant to oxime reactivation (Fleisher & Harris, 1965). The ineffectiveness of therapeutically administered oxime as a treatment for some nerve agents explains the continued research efforts aimed at alternative approaches to protection. In particular, efforts have focused on approaches that prevent the critical enzyme, AChE, from becoming inhibited in the first place. Although the currently used therapy is able to protect soldiers against the lethal effects of nerve agents, it does not adequately protect against the incapacitation that results from high levels of nerve agent exposure. Furthermore, it appears that greater than marginal improvement of these pharmacological approaches will not be possible, because stronger drugs or higher doses are likely to produce unacceptable performance decrements.

NERVE AGENT BIOSCAVENGERS: AN ALTERNATIVE TO CONVENTIONAL APPROACHES

Although successful in protecting against death, current treatments for nerve agent poisoning always result in the victim suffering a toxic insult that subsequently must be therapeutically managed. In contrast, recent efforts have focused on identifying proteins that can act as biological scavengers of organophosphorus compounds and can remain stable in circulation for long periods of time. This novel approach avoids the side effects associated with current antidotes and the requirement for their rapid administration by prophylactically inactivating (through sequestration or hydrolysis) organophosphorus agents before they can react with the target enzyme AChE. The time frame for this inactivation to occur before endogenous AChE is affected is quite narrow (estimated to be approximately 1 min in humans; Talbot, Anderson, Harris, Yarbrough, & Lennox, 1988), so the scavenger function must be very rapid, irreversible, and fastidious. Ideally, the scavenger would enjoy a long residence time in the blood stream, would be biologically inert in the absence of nerve agent, and would not present an antigenic challenge to the immune system. For these reasons, prime efforts to identify candidate bioscavengers have focused on enzymes of mammalian (specifically human) origin.

Candidate bioscavenger proteins, which must be capable of reacting quickly, specifically, and irreversibly with organophosphorus compounds, function generally either by stoichiometrically binding one or two molecules of the nerve agent or by catalyzing the breakdown of these molecules into biologically inert products. In the stoichiometric category are naturally occurring human proteins that bind nerve agents, including enzymes such as cholinesterases and carboxylesterases, as well as antibodies specific for nerve agent haptens. Although this approach is theoretically viable, it has a disadvantage in that the extent of protection is directly proportional to the concentration of unexposed, active scavenger in the bloodstream at the time of nerve agent exposure. Thus, a high concentration of scavenger protein in circulation is necessary to protect against exposure to multiple LD_{50}s of nerve agent.

Candidate enzymes with bona fide catalytic activity against nerve agents have been identified and include human paraoxonase (hu-Pon). In addition, the generation of antibodies with catalytic activity suggests such antibodies could be effective bioscavengers (Brimfield, Lenz, Maxwell, & Broomfield, 1993). Finally, the ability to engineer site-specific amino acid substitutions into naturally occurring scavenger enzymes can allow investigators to alter the binding or catalytic activities of these enzymes. In general, the use of scavengers with catalytic activity would be advantageous because small amounts of enzyme, meaning lower concentrations in circulation, would be sufficient to catalyze the hydrolysis of large amounts of a nerve agent.

By nearly all criteria, the use of biological scavengers, either stoichiometric or catalytic, as a prophylactic approach to provide protection against an exposure to a lethal dose of a nerve agent offers numerous advantages over conventional treatment therapies: (a) The need to have precise knowledge about the timing of exposure to nerve agents in a crisis situation is greatly reduced if not eliminated; (b) the need to administer, repetitively, a host of pharmacologically active drugs with a short duration of action is all but precluded; and (c) the potential for having to use protective clothing and equipment or Military Oriented Protective Posture gear (see Krueger & Banderet, 1997) is greatly reduced. Finally, with the appropriate scavenger(s), such an approach affords protection against all of the current threat agents, including those that are refractory to treatment by atropine and oxime therapy.

STOICHIOMETRIC SCAVENGERS AND THE PROTECTION THEY OFFER

Antibodies

The concept of using a protein that can react with a nerve agent, either stoichiometrically or catalytically, is not new. Over 25 years ago, efforts were undertaken to protect animals by actively immunizing them with analogues of paraoxon or soman attached to appropriate protein carrier molecules to elicit an antibody response against these two highly toxic organophosphorus compounds (Lenz et al., 1984; Sternberger et al., 1972). Rabbits that developed antibodies against paraoxon were protected against exposure to 2 to 3 LD_{50}s of paraoxon (Sternberger, Cuculis, Meyer, Lenz, & Kavanagh, 1974). Significantly, the protected animals were essentially asymptomatic and did not require the administration of any additional therapeutic drugs. Because rabbits immunized with an analogue of soman were not protected against the administration of a lethal dose of that compound, it was determined that the polyclonal antibodies induced in these animals were not of sufficiently high affinity to successfully compete with AChE for the binding of soman (Lenz et al., 1984).

Based on these limited but promising results, efforts were made to generate high-affinity monoclonal antibodies that could be used to afford passive protection against nerve agents. Hunter, Lenz, Brimfield, and Naylor (1982) reported the production of the first antisoman monoclonal antibodies, which were subsequently shown to be of sufficiently high affinity to compete with AChE for soman binding in vitro (Lenz et al., 1984). When mice were passively immunized with these antibodies, they failed to show any protection against the in vivo toxicity of soman, although the time to death was almost doubled in the animals pretreated with the antibody (Lenz et al., 1984). Further in vitro characterization of the monoclonal antibodies showed that their antisoman binding constants were only in the micromolar range but that they were highly soman-specific in that they did not bind the structurally related nerve agent sarin (Brimfield et al., 1985). Subsequent calculations suggest that, to afford protection as a stoichiometric scavenger of soman or sarin, a monoclonal antibody would have to have a binding constant at least 20-fold lower than those of previously characterized antibodies (Lenz, Brimfield, & Cook, 1997).

Enzymes

As shown in Table 1, a number of different enzymes have been tested for their ability to provide protection against nerve agent poisoning. Wolfe, Rush, Doctor, Koplovitz, and Jones (1987) first reported the use of exogenously administered AChE as a bioscavenger when fetal bovine serum acetylcholinesterase (FBS-AChE) was administered to mice 20 hr before a multiple LD_{50} challenge of VX was administered. Complete protection was afforded against a 2 LD_{50} dose of VX (100% survival of exposed animals), whereas moderate protection (80% survival rate) was observed after a 3 LD_{50} challenge. No protection was observed against higher multiple LD_{50} challenges of VX. When animals pretreated with FBS-AChE were exposed to soman, little protection was afforded. However, FBS-AChE pretreatment in conjunction with postexposure atropine and 2-PAM treatment protected mice from 2 LD_{50}s of soman. Wolfe et al. reported that animals displayed no detectable side effects in response to administration of FBS-AChE.

Broomfield et al. (1991) subsequently reported that equine butyrylcholinesterase (eq-BuChE) afforded complete protection against a 2 LD_{50} challenge dose of soman in rhesus monkeys with no supporting therapy and against 3 to 4 LD_{50} doses when atropine was also administered (postexposure). Protection against a single LD_{50} dose of sarin was also demonstrated. In all cases there were no fatalities. Furthermore, when animals were assessed for behavioral deficits using a serial probe recognition (SPR) task (discussed in detail later), they all returned to baseline performance within 9 hr after soman exposure.

Maxwell et al. (1992) carried out a similar set of experiments using rhesus monkeys pretreated with the scavenger FBS-AChE. When monkeys pretreated with FBS-AChE were challenged with either 1.5 or 2.5 LD_{50}s of soman, there were no fatalities or decrements in performance on the SPR task as compared with animals treated with FBS-AChE alone. The animals were also monitored for the generation of an antibody response against the administered FBS-AChE, which might decrease scavenger activity or cause more rapid clearance of FBS-AChE from circulation, or both, but none was detected. Maxwell et al. cautioned, however, that whenever a foreign protein is administered to an animal, the potential for an antibody-mediated immune response must be assessed on a case-by-case basis. Maxwell, Brecht, Doctor, and Wolfe (1993) also compared the relative protection against soman afforded to mice by three different treatments: pyridostigmine pretreatment with atropine therapy postexposure, postexposure oxime (HI-6) and atropine therapy, or FBS-AChE pretreatment alone. They concluded that the FBS-AChE pretreatment offered superior protection against both soman toxicity (survival after 8–10 LD_{50} doses) and behavioral incapacitation.

In a related study, Wolfe et al. (1992) assessed the ability of pretreatment with either FBS-AChE or eq-BuChE to protect rhesus monkeys against multiple LD_{50} doses of soman. Survival and the ability to perform a different behavioral test, the primate equilibrium platform (PEP) task (discussed in detail later), were the variables assessed. Those animals that received FBS-AChE as a pretreatment were protected against a cumulative exposure of 5 LD_{50}s of soman and showed no decrement in the PEP task. These results were reviewed and expanded upon by Doctor et al. (1993), wherein mice pretreated with FBS-AChE were also administered the oxime HI-6 immediately postexposure to sarin. In theory, the oxime will continuously regenerate the inhibited scavenger enzyme in vivo; this approach is predicted to increase the amount of sarin that could be scavenged by a given amount of AChE, making this stoichiometric scavenger "pseudocatalytic." The therapeutic addition of HI-6 after pretreatment with FBS-AChE was found to enhance the efficacy of the scavenger enzyme against sarin in vivo, increasing the ratio of neutralized organophosphorus compound per FBS-AChE molecule from 1:1 (in the presence of AChE alone) to roughly 65:1.

Maxwell, Wolfe, Ashani, and Doctor (1991) identified carboxylesterase (CaE) as another enzyme with the potential to be a good antiorganophosphorus scavenger

TABLE 1
Protection From Organophosphorus Intoxication by Stoichiometric Bioscavengers

Bioscavenger	*Test Species*	*Nerve Agent*	*Protection (LD_{50})*[a]	*Serum $T_{1/2}$*[b]	*Reference*
Polyclonal antibodies[c]	Rabbit	Paraoxon	2–3	Days to weeks	Sternberger et al. (1974)
Polyclonal antibodies[c]	Rabbit	GD	—	Days to weeks	Sternberger et al. (1974)
Monoclonal antibody[c]	Mouse	GD	—/extended mean survival time	6–8 days	Lenz et al. (1984), Vieira & Rajewsky (1988)
FBS-AChE	Rhesus monkey	GD	2–5	30–40 hr	Maxwell et al. (1992), Wolfe et al. (1992)
FBS-AChE	Mouse	GD	2 (with atropine plus 2-PAM)	40–50 hr	Wolfe et al. (1987)
FBS-AChE	Mouse	GD	2 (after CBDP treatment)	Approx. 24 hr	Doctor et al. (1991)
FBS-AChE	Mouse	GD	2–8	24–26 hr	Ashani et al. (1991), Maxwell et al. (1991), Maxwell et al. (1993)
FBS-AChE	Mouse	MEPQ	4	Approx. 24 hr	Doctor et al. (1991), Maxwell et al. (1991)
FBS-AChE	Mouse	VX	2–3.6	Approx. 24–50 hr	Doctor et al. (1991), Maxwell et al. (1991), Wolfe et al. (1987)
eq-BuChE	Rhesus monkey	GB	1	Approx. 26 days	Broomfield et al. (1991)
eq-BuChE	Rhesus monkey	GD	2 (4 with atropine)	Approx. 26 days	Broomfield et al. (1991)
eq-BuChE	Rhesus monkey	GD	5	30–40 hr	Wolfe et al. (1992)

hu-BuChE	Rhesus monkey	GD	2	Approx. 30 hr	Raveh et al. (1997)
hu-BuChE	Rhesus monkey	VX	1.5	Approx. 30 hr	Raveh et al. (1997)
hu-BuChE	Rat	GD	2–3	46 hr	Raveh et al. (1993)
hu-BuChE	Rat	VX	2	46 hr	Raveh et al. (1993)
hu-BuChE	Mouse	GD	2.1	21 hr	Raveh et al. (1997)
hu-BuChE	Mouse	GB	1.6	21 hr	Raveh et al. (1997)
hu-BuChE	Mouse	GA	1.8	21 hr	Raveh et al. (1997)
hu-BuChE	Mouse	VX	4.9	21 hr	Raveh et al. (1997)
CaE[d]	Mouse	GD	16	N.D.[e]	Maxwell et al. (1987)
CaE[d]	Guinea pig	GD	3.5	N.D.[e]	Maxwell et al. (1987)
CaE[d]	Rabbit	GD	3	N.D.[e]	Maxwell et al. (1987)
CaE[d]	Rat	GD	8–9	N.D.[e]	Maxwell et al. (1992), Maxwell (1987)
CaE[d]	Rat	GB	8	N.D.[e]	Maxwell (1992)
CaE[d]	Rat	GA	4–5	N.D.[e]	Maxwell (1992)
CaE[d]	Rat	VX	1	N.D.[e]	Maxwell (1992)
CaE[d]	Rat	Paraoxon	2	N.D.[e]	Maxwell (1992)

Note. N.D. = not determined.

[a]Values represent multiples of median lethal doses (LD_{50}s) of nerve agent survived after scavenger administration. [b]Half-life of scavenger in blood circulation. [c]Polyclonal antibodies are the endogenous serum titer after priming with nerve agent analogues. Monoclonal antibody is produced in vitro by a hybridoma, then passively administered to naïve mice. [d]For each species, the activity of the host's endogenous CaE was tested. [e]Because CaE is an endogenous serum protein, the protection it offers was measured by comparing LD_{50} values in untreated and CBDP-treated animals; 2 mg/kg CBDP completely abolishes endogenous CaE activity (Maxwell, 1992).

molecule. Although AChE and BuChE were found to be more efficient scavengers for soman in mice than CaE, the latter enzyme was capable of affording equal protection on a molar basis. A more detailed discussion of the relative merits of FBS-AChE, human-BuChE, and plasma CaE as scavengers, which describes the extent of protection they offer against a variety of nerve agents both in vitro and in vivo in mice, was presented by Doctor, Raveh, Wolfe, Maxwell, and Ashani (1991). Doctor et al. noted that some of the in vivo noticeable differences in sensitivity and protection may be due to variations in the circulatory pharmacodynamics of the different organophosphorus compounds, such that those inhibitors that distribute more slowly from circulation are more readily scavenged. The extent of protection afforded by FBS-AChE against soman in marmosets and rhesus monkeys with respect to survival was found to be the same in both species, suggesting a similar response can be obtained in humans. None of the animals pretreated with scavenger displayed any adverse symptoms following a LD_{100} challenge dose of soman.

Ultimately, the goal of research on scavenger molecules is to generate a means to protect humans from the toxic effects of nerve agents. In an effort to minimize any physiological, immunological, or psychological side effects of scavenger use in humans, research efforts have begun to focus on the use of human BuChE (hu-BuChE), human CaE, or FBS-AChE (which does not induce an immune response in rhesus monkeys; Maxwell et al., 1992), or all of these. In a series of studies, Ashani and his coworkers (Ashani et al., 1991; Raveh, Grauer, Grunwald, Cohen, & Ashani, 1997; Raveh et al., 1993) examined the scavenger properties of FBS-AChE and particularly hu-BuChE in mice, rats, and rhesus monkeys with respect to several different nerve agents as well as to other organophosphorus compounds. They found that following administration of exogenous cholinesterase, there was a linear correlation between the concentration of cholinesterase in the blood and the level of protection against organophosphorus poisoning. Furthermore, the extent of protection granted to mice was sufficient to counteract multiple LD_{50} doses of soman. When the protective effect of pretreatment with hu-BuChE was compared in mice and rats, it was found that, in both species, the same linear correlation existed between blood concentration of hu-BuChE and protection against soman, sarin, or VX (see Table 1). They further noted that, to be effective, a scavenger had to be present before exposure to the organophosphorus compound because the nerve agent had to be scavenged within the time period of one blood circulation (Raveh et al., 1993). In the final paper in this series, Raveh et al. (1997) reported similar protection results against 3.3 LD_{50}s of soman or 2.1 LD_{50}s of VX in rhesus monkeys. They also reported considerable protection against soman-induced behavioral deficits in a spatial discrimination task.

Catalytic Bioscavengers

In addition to enzymes that act solely as stoichiometric scavengers, there also exist a number of naturally occurring enzymes that are capable of catalyzing the hydrolysis of organophosphorus nerve agents. The phosphotriesterase from *Pseudomonas diminuta* (Sedar & Gibson, 1985) or the human paraoxonase (hu-Pon; Gan, Smolen, Eckerson, & La Du, 1991) have intrinsic catalytic antiorganophosphorus activity. The former enzyme has been shown to afford protection against soman lethality in mice and to protect against behavioral side effects (Broomfield, 1993). However, because this bacterially derived enzyme has no known mammalian homologues, it will likely be a potent initiator of immune responses and is therefore unlikely to serve as an effective prophylactic scavenger. Nonetheless, the *Pseudomonas diminuta* phosphotriesterase could be used as a one-time pretreatment either in addition to or in place of conventional therapy because, in the short term, this enzyme is highly effective against GD, GB, and VX (Dumas, Durst, Landis, Rauschel, & Wild, 1990) and alone induces no known side effects. The hu-Pon enzyme has been identified as having a similar potential for affording protection but without the complication of inducing an immune response (being an endogenous self-antigen in humans); this enzyme has not yet been tested for efficacy in a mammalian model system (Masson et al., 1998).

As well as searching for naturally occurring enzymes with appropriate catalytic activity, several research groups have introduced amino acid changes into existing stoichiometric enzymes in attempts to engineer novel catalytic bioscavengers. The human form of the BuChE gene has been mutated such that the resulting enzyme has catalytic antinerve agent activity (Lockridge et al., 1997; Millard, Lockridge, & Broomfield, 1995, 1998); likewise, the hu-Pon and human CaE are the focus of current efforts to generate catalytic antinerve agent enzymes through site-specific mutation. Finally, as noted previously, it has been possible to immunize mice and recover hybridomas whose antibodies display catalytic activity towards soman (Brimfield et al., 1993; Yli-Kauhaluoma, Humppi, & Yliniemela, 1999). Such catalytic antibodies could be altered to resemble normal human antibodies more closely, thus reducing their immunologic antigenicity (Hale et al., 1988) and prolonging their serum half-life (Vieira & Rajewsky, 1988). Even though most of these enzymes have not yet been tested in mammalian systems, they are indicative of the types of drugs that may soon be available for use in animals and humans. Because mutated BuChE and hu-Pon are based on human proteins, and catalytic antibodies can be rendered predominantly human in structure, the expectation is that these proteins alone would have no physiological side effects. However, behavioral psychologists need to bear in mind that they may have to design tests capable of determining the behavioral side effects, if any, of elevated levels of naturally occurring proteins (and mutant forms thereof) in the circulatory system in order to demonstrate safety of such material to regulatory agencies.

BEHAVIORAL EFFECTS

A discussion of the behavioral effects of biological scavengers falls logically into three parts: first, a review of the behavioral effects, if any, conferred by the scavenger itself when given to an animal in the absence of any cholinesterase inhibitor; second, a consideration of the behavioral effects that result after pretreatment with a biological scavenger followed by exposure to a nerve agent; and third, a comparison of the extent of behavioral side effects that ensue from pretreatment with the scavenger followed by nerve agent exposure versus exposure to a nerve agent followed by conventional therapy. As summarized in Tables 1 and 2, data are available to address each of these situations in several animal species with several different nerve agents.

Behavioral Effects of Scavengers Alone

Most studies that have examined the behavioral effects of biological scavengers have done so by comparing a behavior before scavenger administration, after administration, and then after exposure to nerve agents. Such studies are discussed in the following sections. There are, however, several studies that have examined the behavioral effects of the biological scavengers themselves in the absence of cholinesterase inhibitors. In a study by Genovese and Doctor (1995), rats were trained to perform three behavioral paradigms: a passive avoidance task, a motor activity, and a scheduled-controlled behavior. The performance of animals before and after administration of purified eq-BuChE at a dose that would be expected to provide protection against an exposure of several LD_{50}s of an organophosphorus compound was assessed. The study determined the pharmacokinetic profile of eq-BuChE in rats and then examined the behavior of the animals in the passive–avoidance task when the levels of administered eq-BuChE were maximal. Subsequently, the animals were tested after enzyme levels had started to diminish to enhance the opportunity of detecting any behavioral effects.

During the activity tests, individually housed animals were first allowed to habituate in the test environment. Enzyme was given such that maximum enzyme levels would occur about 1 hr before the beginning of the dark cycle. Motor activity was then monitored for 10 days. As a final test, the effects of excess enzyme were examined in rats trained to perform a VI56s schedule of food reinforcement. Previously, cholinergic compounds had been shown to disrupt performance of this task. Animals were observed for 10 days to ensure that any prolonged or delayed effects would be noted. In all cases for all test paradigms, Genovese and Doctor (1995) reported that eq-BuChE did not disrupt performance of any of the learned tasks, did not upset the circadian cycle of light and dark activity, and had no effect on motor activity. They noted that these outcomes were in contrast to those observed when the standard cholinolytic—atropine—was administered. Finally, they evaluated the protective effects of the levels of enzyme given to the rats in the behavioral studies against 7-(methylethoxyphosphinyloxy)-1-methylquinolinium oxide (MEPQ), a peripherally active organophosphorus compound. Although the level of protection observed was lower than the theoretical prediction, Genovese and Doctor suggested that the simultaneous administration of scavenger and MEPQ might have reduced the efficacy of the administered eq-BuChE.

In a separate study also using eq-BuChE (Matzke, Oubre, Caranto, Gentry, & Galbicka, 1999), rhesus monkeys were trained to perform a serial probe recognition (SPR) task. Using a six-object list, the monkeys were tested for same–different discrimination and delayed same–different discrimination. Once the animals became proficient at the task (80% correct for three successive sessions on 3 consecutive days), they received eq-BuChE in a dose similar to that reported by Broomfield et al. (1991) as sufficient to afford protection against a 2 or 3 LD_{50} soman challenge (vide supra). Matzke et al. reported that repeated administration of commercially prepared eq-BuChE had no effect on the behavior of the monkeys as measured by the SPR studies. Given the lack of behavioral effects and the relatively long in vivo half-life of the eq-BuChE, they concluded that this biological scavenger was potentially more effective than current chemotherapeutic treatments for organophosphorus intoxication.

Behavioral Effects of Scavenger and Nerve Agent Exposure

Studies on the behavioral effects from nerve agent exposure of animals pretreated with biological scavengers tend to fall into two categories: studies in rodents and a relatively large body of data from nonhuman primates. The rodent data are, for the most part, limited to observations of animals after the experimental procedure (Ashani et al., 1991; Maxwell et al., 1991; Raveh et al., 1993) or to the ability of mice to respond to an inverted screen test (Broomfield, 1993; Wolfe et al., 1987). Maxwell et al. (1993) applied a mixture of tests including the inverted screen test as well as activity and motor function assays to mice given FBS-AChE. In all of these studies, the researchers reported that animals pretreated with a scavenger, such as FBS-AChE, eq-BuChE, or hu-BuChE, followed by exposure to soman or VX, exhibited no deficits in behavior. In sharp contrast, animals that received no pretreatment all suffered notable impairment, and the time for recovery took days or longer.

In a more comprehensive study, Brandeis, Raveh, Grunwald, Cohen, and Ashani (1993) examined the effects of soman on rats that either had or had not been pretreated with hu-BuChE. Because organophosphorus intoxication has been identified as causing neuronal degeneration of the hippocampus, rats were trained to perform the Morris water maze (MWM) behavioral task. The MWM, a spatial orientation task, was chosen because this test is a very sensitive assay for the presence of hippocampal lesions. In the MWM, rats are trained to swim in a pool of water until they find a platform submerged below the surface of the water. Rats given a sublethal dose of soman alone had significant impairments in cognitive

TABLE 2
Protection From Behavioral Deficits by Bioscavengers or Conventional Therapy

Protection	*Test Species*	*Toxin*	*Dose (LD_{50})*[a]	*Behavioral Test(s)*	*Impairment*[b]	*Recovery Time*[c]	*Reference*
Without nerve agents							
Atropine	Rat	None	0	Passive avoidance, VI56s schedule	Total	> 1 week	Genovese and Doctor (1995)
eq-BuChE	Rat	None	0	Passive avoidance, motor activity, VI56s schedule	None	Immediate	Genovese and Doctor (1995)
hu-BuChE	Rat	None	0	MWM	None	Immediate	Brandeis et al. (1993)
Pyridostigmine	Rhesus monkey	None	0	PEP	Substantial	N.D.	Blick et al. (1994)
eq-BuChE	Rhesus monkey	None	0	SPR	None	Immediate	Matzke et al. (1999)
eq-BuChE	Rhesus monkey	None	0	Observation, SPR	Subtle SPR defect	Approx. 6 days	Castro et al. (1993)
eq-BuChE	Rhesus monkey	None	0	Observation, SPR	None	Immediate	Matzke et al. (1999)
hu-BuChE	Rhesus monkey	None	0	SD	Minor (one fourth had errors)	> 1 day	Raveh et al. (1997)
With nerve agents							
Pyridostigmine and atropine	Mouse	GD	8	Inverted screen, motor function, lacrimation, and activity level	Near total	N.D.	Maxwell et al. (1993)
HI-6 and atropine	Mouse	GD	8	Inverted screen, motor function, lacrimation, and activity level	Near total	N.D.	Maxwell et al. (1993)
FBS-AChE	Mouse	GD	8	Inverted screen, motor function, lacrimation, and activity level	Very minor	N.D.	Maxwell et al. (1993)
FBS-AChE	Mouse	VX	2–3	Inverted screen	Minor (one tenth failed)	N.D.	Wolfe et al. (1987)

PTE[d]	Mouse	GD	3–4	Inverted screen	None	Immediate	Broomfield (1993)
eq-BuChE	Rat	MEPQ	> 1	VI56s schedule	Moderate (70% of control)[e]	N.D.	Genovese and Doctor (1995)
hu-BuChE	Rat	GD	1.5	Observation	Minor (tremors in one sixth)	3 hr	Raveh et al. (1993)
hu-BuChE	Rat	VX	1.4	Observation	None	Immediate	Raveh et al. (1993)
hu-BuChE	Rat	GD	1.5	MWM	None	Immediate	Brandeis et al. (1993)
FBS-AChE	Rhesus monkey	GD	5	Observation, PEP	None	Immediate	Wolfe et al. (1992)
FBS-AChE	Rhesus monkey	GD	2.7	Observation, SPR	None	Immediate	Maxwell et al. (1992)
eq-BuChE	Rhesus monkey	GD	2	Observation, SPR	Transient	Rapid (8–16 hr)	Broomfield et al. (1991)
eq-BuChE	Rhesus monkey	GD	2	Observation, SPR	Subtle SPR defect[f]	Approx. 6 days	Castro et al. (1994)
eq-BuChE	Rhesus monkey	GD	4	Observation, PEP	None	Immediate	Wolfe et al. (1992)
hu-BuChE	Rhesus monkey	GD	3.3	SD	Minor (one fourth had errors)	Approx. 5 days	Raveh et al. (1997)
Pyridostigmine	Rhesus monkey	GD	Approx. 0.4	Observation, PEP	Substantial	> 1 day	Blick et al. (1994)
Pyridostigmine, atropine, and 2-PAM	Rhesus monkey	GD	2	Observation, SPR	Substantial	> 2 weeks	Broomfield et al. (1991)
Pyridostigmine, atropine, and 2-PAM	Rhesus monkey	GD	5	Observation, SPR	Substantial	> 2 weeks	Castro et al. (1991)
Pyridostigmine, atropine, 2-PAM, and diazepam	Rhesus monkey	GD	5	Observation, SPR	Substantial	6 days	Castro et al. (1991)

Note. MWM = Morris water maze; PEP = primate equilibrium platform; SPR = serial probe recognition; SD = spatial discrimination; N.D. = not determined.

[a]Median lethal dose of nerve agent administered. [b]Behavioral impairment relative to untreated animals. [c]Time elasped before performance returns to pretreatment levels. [d]Phosphotriesterase from *Pseudomonas diminuta*. [e]The VI56s behavior is a food-reward–based task. Genovese and Doctor (1995) speculated that nausea caused by nerve agent exposure, rather than a cognitive deficit, may have caused the behavioral impairment. [f]The sustained subtle defect was in addition to the short-term, substantial defect described in Broomfield et al. (1991).

function that manifested itself over a period of several weeks. Pretreatment with hu-BuChE provided substantial protection from these behavioral decrements; the performance of hu-BuChE-pretreated, soman-exposed rats was indistinguishable from that of control rats exposed only to saline. Brandeis et al. also observed that rats that were administered the scavenger in the absence of soman had no impairments in behavioral performance, and they concluded that a scavenger such as hu-BuChE enhances survival as well as alleviates the cognitive dysfunctions that usually follow exposure to nerve agents.

Studies in nonhuman primates have led to similar conclusions. In a pair of studies by Broomfield et al. (1991) and Maxwell et al. (1992), using eq-BuChE and FBS-AChE, respectively, as scavengers, the SPR task was used to evaluate the ability of these two scavengers to protect against behavioral decrements after soman poisoning. In the case of eq-BuChE administered to rhesus monkeys, the scavenger itself had no detrimental effect on SPR performance. After eq-BuChE pretreatment, which was followed by 2 LD_{50}s of soman administered intravenously, animals exhibited a transient performance decrement at 8 hr post-challenge. Thereafter, they returned to baseline performance levels and were followed for up to 6 days. A closer analysis of these data (Castro et al., 1994) revealed a subtle performance diminution, wherein animals responded below criteria when the SPR items were in the middle of a list as opposed to the beginning or the end. This effect was evident even in the absence of soman, suggesting that it had been mediated by administration of eq-BuChE alone. Castro et al. also proposed that, in some cases, a small concentration of soman might gain entry into the CNS even in the presence of a concentration of scavenger sufficient to afford protection on a theoretical molar basis. Subsequently, Matzke et al. (1999; vide supra) reported that administration of eq-BuChE alone had no detectable effect on the performance of animals trained on the SPR task.

In the study by Maxwell et al. (1992) using FBS-AChE as the scavenger in a similar experimental design with SPR as the behavioral task, no decrement in performance was found either due to the scavenger itself or following soman intoxication. A related study in rhesus monkeys trained to perform a PEP task detected no performance decrements in animals given FBS-AChE alone or pretreated with scavenger prior to a cumulative challenge of 4 LD_{50}s of soman. When eq-BuChE was the scavenger, transient performance decrements were observed when the soman challenge exceeded a cumulative dose of 4 LD_{50}s, although all of the animals survived this otherwise lethal dose. In no case were residual or delayed performance effects detected up to 6 weeks after nerve agent exposure in animals pretreated with either cholinesterase. In a similar study by Wolfe et al. (1992), two of four monkeys that received purified eq-BuChE as a pretreatment did show some transient decrement in PEP task performance when exposed to a cumulative dose of greater than 4 LD_{50}s of soman. All of the experimental animals in Wolfe et al.'s study were observed for an additional 6 weeks, yet none displayed any residual or delayed performance decrements. In marked contrast to these results, a more than 14-day recovery time was required to restore baseline performance of the SPR task for monkeys receiving conventional atropine and oxime therapy following exposure to soman (Castro, Larsen, Finger, Solana, & McMaster, 1991; vide infra). A summary of the results from these primate studies can be found in Doctor et al. (1993) and in Doctor et al. (1991).

A recent study by Raveh et al. (1997) described the protective effects of hu-BuChE in rhesus monkeys exposed to soman or VX. The monkeys were first trained on a spatial discrimination (SD) task and then pretreated with hu-BuChE before exposure to the organophosphorus nerve agents. The scavenger afforded protection against the lethality of soman or VX, but with respect to protection against behavioral deficits, the results were mixed. Four monkeys treated with hu-BuChE and subsequently exposed to 3.3 to 4.1 LD_{50}s of soman were tested on the SD task. One animal showed no performance deficit, and one monkey exhibited mild signs of intoxication but resumed performance of the SD task the following day, albeit with an increased error rate. The third animal showed unexpected toxic signs 10 min after soman exposure, became active again 4 hr later, but did not perform the SD task for 2 days (no additional therapy was administered). When this third monkey resumed performance of the task, it displayed increased working memory errors for about 5 days. The fourth monkey was given 4.1 LD_{50}s of soman and developed convulsions and loss of posture. The animal was treated with atropine and TAB (a mixture of the oxime TMB-4, atropine, and benactyzine), recovered quickly, and resumed performance of the task less than 4 hr after soman exposure. This animal exhibited transient behavioral deficits, which Raveh et al. reported to be mild. Despite less than perfect protection against performance decrements, the authors concluded that the hu-BuChE scavenger offered a high level of protection against soman-induced behavioral deficits in the performance of the SD task. Raveh et al. also commented on the consistency of results across species for this type of pretreatment and suggested that it should be possible to predict the extent of protection that would be afforded humans based on their own results and the work of others.

Comparison of the Behavioral Effects of Scavengers Versus Conventional Therapy After Nerve Agent Exposure

The results reported previously using the SPR task as a measure of behavioral performance when scavenger pretreatment was followed by administration of multiple LD_{50}s of soman (Broomfield et al., 1991; Castro et al., 1994; Maxwell et al., 1992) can be compared with similar studies using conventional therapy. One such example (Castro et al., 1991) used the SPR task to assess the extent of behavioral disruption in rhesus monkeys following soman exposure. The animals received pyridostigmine bromide pretreatment and, subsequent to soman exposure, treatment with atropine, the oxime 2-PAM, and in some cases the anticonvulsant diazepam. Pyridostigmine pretreatment alone had no effect on SPR performance in trained animals. Following soman exposure and treatment with atropine and oxime either with or without diazepam, recovery of preexposure performance on the SPR task took from 6 (when coadministered diazepam) to 15 days (without the anticonvulsant). Monkeys that did not receive diazepam exhibited severe convulsive episodes, whereas only one of five monkeys that received diazepam suffered tonic-clonic convulsions. Castro et al. (1991) concluded that diazepam would be an excellent adjunct to the pyridostigmine pretreatment followed by atropine and 2-PAM oxime treatment regimen. Although the value of diazepam as an anticonvulsant treatment drug cannot be ignored, the extent of incapacitation and the prolonged recovery time of 6 to 15 days after conventional therapy contrasts dramatically with the results from bioscavenger prophylaxis. The lack of or, in some cases, the presence of only a subtle, transient decrease in SPR performance when a bioscavenger is used as a pretreatment (Broomfield et al., 1991; Maxwell et al., 1992) offers impressive evidence for the value of this approach as affording protection against behavioral effects following nerve agent poisoning.

DISCUSSION

Organophosphorus nerve agents represent a very real threat not only to soldiers in the field but also to the public at large (Ember, 1991). Nerve agents have already been used by terrorist groups against a civilian population and, due to their low cost and relative ease of synthesis, are likely to be used again in the future (Masuda, Takatsu, Morianari, & Ozawa, 1995). Current therapeutic regimes for nerve agent exposure are generally effective at preventing fatalities if administered in an appropriate time frame. However, due to their requirement for rapid administration, it remains unclear whether under battlefield conditions these therapeutic interventions could be effectively implemented on a large scale. Furthermore, pyridostigmine pretreatment coupled with postexposure administration of an oxime, atropine, and an anticonvulsant does not prevent the substantial behavioral incapacitation or, in some cases, permanent brain damage that can result from organophosphorus poisoning. It is therefore important from the standpoint of military and domestic security to develop new defenses against nerve agents, including the use of bioscavenger molecules, that avoid many of these difficulties. Although the use of nerve agents on the battlefield may be somewhat predictable, their use in a terrorist situation will be, in all probability, a random event. The ability to afford long-term protection for first-responders may be a notable advantage of biological scavengers.

The use of bioscavengers as a defense against organophosphorus intoxication has many advantages and few apparent disadvantages. As discussed in detail previously, bioscavengers can afford protection against not only mortality but also most or all of the adverse physiological and behavioral effects of nerve agent exposure. They can be administered prophylactically, either intravenously or intramuscularly with equal efficacy, precluding the need for immediate postexposure treatment. In addition, the use of bioscavengers has several psychological benefits that are likely to result in a higher degree of user acceptability than exists for conventional therapy. No postexposure autoinjectors are necessary, protection is afforded with little chance of short- or long-term side effects, and the requirement for protective chemical clothing may be reduced. Of particular significance is the fact that current candidate bioscavenger proteins are, for the most part, enzymes of human origin. From a scientific standpoint, these proteins are good candidates because they are less likely to be recognized by cells of the immune system and will enjoy prolonged residence times in circulation. From the point of view of the user, individuals in essence are having their inherent resistance to nerve agents enhanced by using a substance that their bodies already produce, rather than being injected with drugs and enzyme inhibitors that alone can produce potent side-effects.

However, there are several challenges that must be met before bioscavengers can augment or replace the current therapeutic regimes for nerve agent intoxication. First, scavenger proteins, either alone or in combination, with a range of specificities that encompasses all known nerve agents must be defined. The immunogenicity and serum half-life of the scavenger(s) must be determined in humans, and efforts may be required to minimize the former and maximize the latter. Finally, appropriate dosages of scavenger(s) must be determined that will, based on animal models, protect against concentrations of nerve agents likely to be encountered on the battlefield. Although the majority of the research to date has focused on stoichiometric scavengers, the use of either naturally occurring or genetically engineered enzymes with catalytic activity holds the greatest theoretical promise for the development of a broad specificity prophylactic scavenger. Future efforts are likely to focus on generating, characterizing, and employing such enzymes in rodent and nonhuman primate models.

ACKNOWLEDGMENTS

The opinions expressed in this review are those of the authors and should not be construed as those advocated by the U.S. Army Medical Research Institute of Chemical Defense or statements of policy of the U.S. Army or the U.S. Department of Defense. Douglas M. Cerasoli was supported by a National Research Council postdoctoral fellowship.

REFERENCES

Ashani, Y., Shapira, S., Levy, D., Wolfe, A. D., Doctor, B. P., & Raveh, L. (1991). Butyrylcholinesterase and acetylcholinesterase prophylaxis against soman poisoning in mice. *Biochemical Pharmacology, 41,* 37–41.

Bajgar, J., Jakl, A., & Hrdina, V. (1971). Influence of trimedoxime and atropine on acetylcholinesterase activity in some parts of the brain of mice poisoned by isopropylmethyl phosphonofluoridate. *Biochemical Pharmacology, 20,* 3230–3233.

Ballantyne, B., & Marrs, T. C. (1992). Overview of the biological and clinical aspects of organophosphates and carbamates. In B. Ballantyne & T. C. Marrs (Eds.), *Clinical and experimental toxicology of organophosphates and carbamates* (pp. 1–14). Oxford, England: Butterworth.

Bismuth, C., Inns, R. H., & Marrs, T. C. (1992). Efficacy, toxicity and clinical use of oximes in anticholinesterase poisoning. In B. Ballantyne & T. C. Marrs (Eds.), *Clinical and experimental toxicology of organophosphates and carbamates* (pp. 555–577). Oxford, England: Butterworth.

Blick, D. W., Murphy, M. R., Brown, G. C., Yochmowitz, M. G., Fanton, J. W., & Hartgraves, S. L. (1994). Acute behavioral toxicity of pyridostigmine or soman in primates. *Toxicology and Applied Pharmacology, 126,* 311–318.

Brandeis, R., Raveh, L., Grunwald, J., Cohen, E., & Ashani, Y. (1993). Prevention of soman-induced cognitive deficits by pretreatment with human butyrylcholinesterase in rats. *Pharmacology, Biochemistry, and Behavior, 46,* 889–896.

Brimblecombe, R. W. (1977). Drugs acting on central cholinergic mechanisms and affecting respiration. *Pharmacology and Therapeutics, Part B: General and Systematic Pharmacology, 3,* 65–74.

Brimfield, A. A., Hunter, K. W., Lenz, D. E., Benschop, H. P., Van Dijk, C., & De Jong, L. P. A. (1985). Structural and stereochemical specificity of mouse monoclonal antibodies to the organophosphorus cholinesterase inhibitor soman. *Molecular Pharmacology, 28,* 32–39.

Brimfield, A. A., Lenz, D. E., Maxwell, D. M., & Broomfield, C. C. (1993). Catalytic antibodies hydrolyzing organophosphorus esters. *Chemico-Biological Interactions, 87,* 95–102.

Broomfield, C. A. (1993). A purified recombinant organophosphorus acid anhydrase protects mice against soman. *Chemico-Biological Interactions, 87,* 279–284.

Broomfield, C. A., Maxwell, D. M., Solana, R. P., Castro, C. A., Finger, A. V., & Lenz, D. E. (1991). Protection of butyrylcholinesterase against organophosphorus poisoning in nonhuman primates. *Journal of Pharmacology and Experimental Therapeutics, 259,* 633–638.

Castro, C. A., Gresham, V. C., Finger, A. V., Maxwell, D. M., Solana, R. P., Lenz, D. E., et al. (1994). Behavioral decrements persist in rhesus monkeys trained on a serial probe recognition task despite protection against soman lethality by butyrylcholinesterase. *Neurotoxicology and Teratology, 16,* 145–148.

Castro, C. A., Larsen, T., Finger, A. V., Solana, R., & McMaster, S. B. (1991). Behavioral efficacy of diazepam against nerve agent exposure in rhesus monkeys. *Pharmacology, Biochemistry, and Behavior, 41,* 159–164.

Chabrier, P. E., & Jacob, J. (1980). In vivo and in vitro inhibition of cholinesterase by methyl-1 (S methyl phosphoryl-3) imidazolium (MSPI), a model of an "instantly" aged phosphorylated enzyme. *Archives of Toxicology, 45,* 15–20.

Clement, J. G. (1982). HI-6 reactivation of central and peripheral acetylcholinesterase following inhibition by soman, sarin and tabun in vivo in the rat. *Biochemical Pharmacology, 31,* 1283–1287.

Dacre, J. C. (1984). Toxicology of some anticholinesterases used as chemical warfare agents—A review. In M. Brzin, E. A. Barnard, & D. Sket (Eds.), *Cholinesterases, fundamental and applied aspects* (pp. 415–426). Berlin, Germany: de Gruyter.

de Candole, C. A., Douglas, W. W., Evans, C. L., Holmes, R., Spencer, K. E. V., Torrance, R. W., et al. (1953). The failure of respiration in death by anticholinesterase poisoning. *British Journal of Pharmacology and Chemotherapy, 6,* 466–475.

Doctor, B. P., Blick, D. W., Caranto, G., Castro, C. A., Gentry, M. K., Larison, R., et al. (1993). Cholinesterases as scavengers for organophosphorus compounds: Protection of primate performance against soman toxicity. *Chemico-Biological Interactions, 87,* 285–293.

Doctor, B. P., Raveh, L., Wolfe, A. D., Maxwell, D. M., & Ashani, Y. (1991). Enzymes as pretreatment drugs for organophosphate toxicity. *Neuroscience and Biobehavioral Reviews, 15,* 123–128.

Dumas, D. P., Durst, H. D., Landis, W. G., Raushel, F. M., & Wild, J. R. (1990). Inactivation of organophosphorus nerve agents by the phosphotriesterase from *Pseudomonas diminuta. Archives of Biochemistry and Biophysics, 277,* 155–159.

Dunn, M. A., & Sidell, F. R. (1989). Progress in medical defense against nerve agents. *Journal of the American Medical Association, 262,* 649–652.

Ember, L. (1991, August 19). Chemical weapons: Plans prepared to destroy Iraqi arms. *Chemical Engineering News,* pp. 6–7.

Erdmann, W., Bosse, I., & Franke, P. (1965). Zur Resorption und Ausscheidung von Toxigonin nach Intramuskularer am Menschen [The absorption and elimination of toxigonin after intramuscular injection in humans]. *Deutsche Medizinische Wochenschrift, 90,* 1436–1438.

Fleisher, J. H., & Harris, L. W. (1965). Dealkylation as a mechanism for aging of cholinesterase after poisoning with pinacolyl methylphosphonofluoridate. *Biochemical Pharmacology, 14,* 641–650.

Gan, K. N., Smolen, A., Eckerson, H. W., & La Du, B. N. (1991). Purification of human serum paraoxonase/arylesterase. *Drug Metabolism and Disposition, 19,* 100–106.

Genovese, R. F., & Doctor, B. P. (1995). Behavioral and pharmacological assessment of butyrylcholinesterase in rats. *Pharmacology, Biochemistry, and Behavior, 51,* 647–654.

Gordon, J. J., Leadbeater, L., & Maidment, M. P. (1978). The protection of animals against organophosphorus poisoning by pretreatment with a carbamate. *Toxicology and Applied Pharmacology, 43,* 207–216.

Hale, G., Dyer, M. J. S., Clark, M. R., Phillips, J. M., Marcus, R., Reichmann, L., et al. (1988). Remission induction in non-Hodgkins lyphoma with reshaped human monoclonal antibody CAMPATH-1H. *Lancet,* 2(8625), 1394–1399.

Heath, A. J. W., & Meredith, T. (1992). Atropine in the management of anticholinesterase poisoning. In B. Ballantyne & T. C. Marrs (Eds.), *Clinical and experimental toxicology of organophosphates and carbamates* (pp. 543–554). Oxford, England: Butterworth.

Heffron, P. F., & Hobbinger, F. (1979). Relationship between inhibition of acetylcholinesterase and response of the rat phrenic nerve-diaphragm preparation to indirect stimulation at higher frequencies. *British Journal of Pharmacology, 66,* 323–329.

Huff, B. B. (Ed.). (1986). *Physician's desk reference.* Oradell, NJ: Medical Economics.

Hunter, K. W., Lenz, D. E., Brimfield, A. A., & Naylor, J. A. (1982). Quantification of the organophosphorus nerve agent soman by competitive inhibition enzyme immunoassay using monoclonal antibodies. *Federation of European Biochemical Societies Letters,* 22(149), 147–151.

Koelle, G. B. (1963). Cholinesterases and anticholinesterase agents. In O. Eichler & A. Farah (Eds.), *Handbuch der Experimentellen Pharmakologie* (Vol. 15). Berlin, Germany: Springer-Verlag.

Krueger, G. P., & Banderet, L. E. (1997). Effects of chemical protective clothing on military performance: A review of the issues. *Military Psychology, 9,* 251–253.

Leadbeater, L., Inns, R. H., & Rylands, J. M. (1985). Treatment of soman poisoning. *Toxicology and Applied Pharmacology, 5*(6, Pt. 2), 225–231.

Lenz, D. E., Brimfield, A. A., & Cook, L. A. (1997). The development of immunoassays for detection of chemical warfare agents. In D. Aga & E. M. Thurman (Eds.), *Development and applications of immunoassays for environmental analysis* (pp. 77–86). Washington, DC: ACS Books.

Lenz, D. E., Brimfield, A. A., Hunter, K. W., Benschop, H. P., De Jong, L. P. A., Van Dijk, C., et al. (1984). Studies using a monoclonal antibody against soman. *Fundamental and Applied Toxicology, 4*(2, Pt. 2), 156–164.

Lockridge, O., Blong, R. M., Masson, P., Froment, M.-T., Millard, C. B., & Broomfield, C. A. (1997). A single amino acid substitution, Gly117His, confers phosphotriesterase (organophosphorus acid anhydride hydrolase) activity on human butyrylcholinesterase. *Biochemistry, 36,* 786–795.

Masson, P., Josse, D., Lockridge, O., Viguié, N., Taupin, C., & Buhler, C. (1998). Enzymes hydrolyzing organophosphates as potential catalytic scavengers against organophosphate poisoning. *Journal of Physiology, 92,* 357–362.

Masuda, A. N., Takatsu, M., Morianari, H., & Ozawa, T. (1995). Sarin poisoning in Tokyo subway. *Lancet, 345,* 1446.

Matzke, S. M., Oubre, J. L., Caranto, G. R., Gentry, M. K., & Galbicka, G. (1999). Behavioral and immunological effects of exogenous butyrylcholinesterase in rhesus monkeys. *Pharmacology, Biochemistry, and Behavior, 62,* 523–530.

Maxwell, D. M. (1992). The specificity of carboxylesterase protection against the toxicity of organophosphorus compounds. *Toxicology and Applied Pharmacology, 114,* 306–312.

Maxwell, D. M., Brecht, K. M., Doctor, B. P., & Wolfe, A. D. (1993). Comparison of antidote protection against soman by pyridostigmine, HI-6 and acetylcholinesterase. *Journal of Pharmacology and Experimental Therapeutics, 264,* 1085–1089.

Maxwell, D. M., Brecht, K. M., & O'Neill, B. L. (1987). The effect of carboxylesterase inhibition on interspecies differences in soman toxicity. *Toxicology Letters, 39,* 35–42.

Maxwell, D. M., Castro, C. A., De La Hoz, D. M., Gentry, M. K., Gold, M. B., Solana, R. P., et al. (1992). Protection of rhesus monkeys against soman and prevention of performance decrement by pretreatment with acetylcholinesterase. *Toxicology and Applied Pharmacology, 115,* 44–49.

Maxwell, D. M., Wolfe, A. D., Ashani, Y., & Doctor, P. B. (1991). Cholinesterase and carboxylesterase as scavengers for organophosphorus agents. In F. Bacu (Ed.), *Proceedings of the Third International Meeting on Cholinesterase* (pp. 206–209). Washington, DC: ACS Books.

Maynard, R. L., & Beswick, F. W. (1992). Organophosphorus compounds as chemical warfare agents. In B. Ballantyne & T. C. Marrs (Eds.), *Clinical and experimental toxicology of organophosphates and carbamates* (pp. 373–385). Oxford, England: Butterworth.

McDonough, J. H. (2002/this issue). Performance impacts of nerve agents and their pharmacological countermeasures. *Military Psychology, 14,* 93–119.

McDonough, J. H., & Penetar, D. M. (1982). The effects of cholinergic blocking agents and anticholinesterase compounds on memory, learning and performance. In M. Y. Spiegelstein & A. Levy (Eds.), *Behavioral models and the analysis of drug action: Proceedings of the 27th OHOLO Conference* (pp. 155–174). Amsterdam: Elsevier.

Millard, C. B., Lockridge, O., & Broomfield, C. A. (1995). Design and expression of organophosphorus acid anhydride hydrolase activity in human butyrylcholinesterase. *Biochemistry, 34,* 15925–15933.

Millard, C. B., Lockridge, O., & Broomfield, C. A. (1998). Organophosphorus acid anhydride hydrolase activity in human butyrylcholinesterase: Synergy results in a somanase. *Biochemistry, 37,* 237–247.

Raveh, L., Grauer, E., Grunwald, J., Cohen, E., & Ashani, Y. (1997). The stoichiometry of protection against soman and VX toxicity in monkeys pretreated with human butyrylcholinesterase. *Toxicology and Applied Pharmacology, 145,* 43–53.

Raveh, L., Grunwald, J., Marcus, D., Papier, Y., Cohen, E., & Ashani, Y. (1993). Human butyrylcholinesterase as a general prophylactic antidote for nerve agent toxicity. *Biochemical Pharmacology, 45,* 2465–2474.

Reiner, E. (1971). Spontaneous reactivation of phosphorylated and carbamylated cholinesterases. *Bulletin of the World Health Organization, 44,* 109–112.

Sedar, C. M., & Gibson, D. T. (1985). Enzymatic hydrolysis of organophosphates: Cloning and expression of a parathion hydrolase gene from *Pseudomonas diminuta. Bio/Technology, 3,* 567–571.

Sidell, F., & Groff, W. (1970). Toxigonin: Blood levels and side effects after intramuscular administration in man. *Journal of Pharmaceutical Sciences, 59,* 793–797.

Somani, S. M., Solana, R. P., & Dube, S. N. (1992). Toxicodynamics of nerve agents. In S. M. Somani (Ed.), *Chemical warfare agents* (pp. 68–124). San Diego, CA: Academic.

Sternberger, L. A., Cuculis, J. J., Meyer, H. G., Lenz, D. E., & Kavanagh, W. G. (1974). Antibodies to organophosphorus haptens: Immunity to paraoxon poisoning. *Federation Proceedings, 33,* 728.

Sternberger, L. A., Sim, V. M., Kavanagh, W. G., Cuculis, J. J., Meyer, H. G., Lenz, D. E., et al. (1972). A vaccine against organophosphorus poisoning. *Army Science Conference Proceedings, 3,* 429–441.

Stewart, W. C. (1959). The effects of sarin and atropine on the respiratory center and neuromuscular junctions of the rat. *Canadian Journal of Biochemistry and Physiology, 37,* 651–660.

Stewart, W. C., & Anderson, E. A. (1968). Effects of a cholinesterase inhibitor when injected into the medulla of the rabbit. *Journal of Pharmacology and Experimental Therapeutics, 162,* 309–318.

Talbot, B. G., Anderson, D. R., Harris, L. W., Yarbrough, L. W., & Lennox, W. J. (1988). A comparison of in vivo and in vitro rates of aging of soman-inhibited erythrocyte acetylcholinesterase in different animal species. *Drug and Chemical Toxicology, 11,* 298–305.

Taylor, P. (1990). Anticholinesterase agents. In A. G. Gilman, T. W. Rall, A. S. Nies, & P. Taylor (Eds.), *The pharmacological basis of therapeutics* (pp. 131–149). New York: Macmillan.

Vieira, P., & Rajewsky, K. (1988). The half-lives of serum immunoglobulins in adult mice. *European Journal of Immunology, 18,* 313–316.

Vojvodic, V. (1970). Blood levels, urinary excretion and potential toxicity of N,N′-trimethylenebis-(pyridinium-4-aldoxime) dichloride (TMB-4) in healthy men following intramuscular injection of the oxime. *Clinical Pharmacology, 2,* 216–220.

Wenger, G. R. (1979). Effects of physostigmine, atropine and scopolamine on behavior maintained by a multiple schedule of food presentation in the mouse. *Journal of Pharmacology and Experimental Therapeutics, 209,* 137–143.

Wiezorek, W., Kreisel, W., Schnitzlein, W., & Matzkowski, H. (1968). Eigenwirkungen von Trimedoxin und Pralidoxim am Menschen [Specific effects of trimedoxin and pralidoxim on humans]. *Zeitschrift Militarmedizine, 4,* 223–226.

Wilson, I. B., & Ginsburg, S. (1955). A powerful reactivator of alkyl phosphate-inhibited acetylcholinesterase. *Biochimica et Biophysica Acta, 18,* 168–170.

Wolfe, A. D., Blick, D. W., Murphy, M. R., Miller, S. A., Gentry, M. K., Hartgraves, S. L., et al. (1992). Use of cholinesterases as pretreatment drugs for the protection of rhesus monkeys against soman toxicity. *Toxicology and Applied Pharmacology, 117,* 189–193.

Wolfe, A. D., Rush, R. S., Doctor, B. P., Koplovitz, I., & Jones, D. (1987). Acetylcholinesterase prophylaxis against organophosphate toxicity. *Fundamental and Applied Toxicology, 9,* 266–270.

Yli-Kauhaluoma, J., Humppi, T., & Yliniemela, A. (1999). Hydrolysis of organophosphorus nerve agent soman by the monoclonal antibodies elicited against an oxyphosphorane hapten. *Acta Chemica Scandinavica, 53,* 473–479.

MILITARY PSYCHOLOGY, 2002, *14*(2), 145–157

Vesicant Agents and Antivesicant Medical Countermeasures: Clinical Toxicology and Psychological Implications

William J. Smith
Biochemical Pharmacology Branch
U.S. Army Medical Research Institute of Chemical Defense
Aberdeen Proving Ground, Maryland

The ability of vesicant agents to produce debilitating cutaneous blisters, respiratory problems, acute visual impairment, or all of these, is well recognized. Their psychological impact on members of the armed forces who are, or who believe they are, at risk of exposure to agents such as mustard gas are much less understood. Therefore, better understanding of the clinical ramifications of exposure, medical assistance that can be given to mustard gas victims, and the long-term sequelae to which casualties might be subject can go a long way toward mitigating warfighter concerns.

Chemicals capable of inducing blisters, known as blistering or vesicating agents, have been widely known for more than 150 years. They were extensively used in chemical warfare during World War I (WWI), well before the development of the more deadly nerve agents 25 years later. Blistering agents continue to be used in present day conflicts for several reasons. They are simple to produce; they cause a large number of incapacitating, nonlethal and lethal injuries; and their persistence after dispersal can prevent an enemy from making use of a contaminated area.

Sulfur mustard (2,2′-dichlorodiethyl sulfide, mustard gas, HD) and lewisite (2-chlorovinyldichloroarsine) are the best known vesicating (blistering) chemical warfare agents. Sulfur mustard is the blistering agent most commonly associated

---

This article is part of a special issue, "Chemical Warfare and Chemical Terrorism: Psychological and Performance Outcomes," of *Military Psychology*, 2002, *14*(2), 83–177.

Requests for reprints should be sent to William J. Smith, USAMRICD, ATTN: MRMC–UV–PB, 3100 Ricketts Point Road, Aberdeen Proving Ground, MD 21010–5400.

with warfare and was the major cause of chemical casualties in WWI (Vedder, 1925). Its use has been documented in regional conflicts over the past 50 years, most recently in the Iran–Iraq conflict of the 1980s in the Middle East (United Nations, 1984, 1986, 1987). In that war, sulfur mustard was the predominant agent involved in causing a reported 45,000 chemical casualties (Carus, 1988) among military and civilian populations (Hay & Robert, 1990; Hu, Cook-Deegan, & Shurki, 1989). Lewisite, in contrast, was not used in WWI, and although it has been stockpiled and incorporated into bombs and artillery shells, no reliable reports have documented its use in combat. Although there were no reported uses of vesicant agents during the Persian Gulf War in 1991, they remain significant threats against U.S. armed forces, and its ability to generate immediate incapacitating eye injury and skin pain make it a potential terrorist weapon. Several reviews of the pharmacology, toxicology, and casualty management of vesicant agents have been published (Papirmeister, Feister, Robinson, & Ford, 1991; Pechura & Rall, 1993; Sidell, Urbanetti, Smith, & Hurst, 1997; W. J. Smith & Dunn, 1991). As an example, dimercaprol (British Anti-Lewisite, BAL) can prevent or ameliorate Lewisite skin and eye lesions if applied topically within minutes of exposure, and intramuscular administration of BAL can reduce systemic effects.

TOXICITY OF MUSTARD

The majority of sulfur mustard casualties experience nonfatal but disabling skin, eye, and respiratory problems—the three key targets affected by exposure to sulfur mustard—often with a prolonged period before full recovery. Physicians familiar with other alkylating agents used in clinical medicine deal mainly with their systemic toxicity to cells of the bone marrow, lymphoid tissue, and gut mucosa because of their normal routes of administration. The fact that wartime sulfur mustard exposure involves external epithelial surfaces rather than primary systemic absorption largely accounts for this important difference in tissues affected. Although heavy battlefield exposure to sulfur mustard may indeed cause the same systemic toxicity encountered with other alkylating compounds, such patients comprise only a small percentage of all mustard casualties. From the accounts of WWI through reports of the most recently managed Middle East casualties in 1988, mortality among all individuals exposed to sulfur mustard has remained between 1% and 5% (Vedder, 1925; Willems, 1989). The primary clinical problems in caring for mustard gas casualties continue to center on the cutaneous, ocular, and respiratory manifestations of exposure to this agent.

Since WWI, a large body of information on sulfur mustard toxicity has been reported from wartime accounts, accidental laboratory and industrial exposures, and animal experiments. Deliberate volunteer exposures of skin to minute amounts of mustard were commonplace in many countries through WWII; however, realization of the potential carcinogenic risk involved in exposure to any DNA-alkylating compound now limits human tissue studies to explants and cell cultures.

Sulfur mustard exposure does not cause any immediately noticeable effects but leads to a slowly evolving lesion that heals after a prolonged period of weeks to months. During the latent period (1 to 8 hr) before a casualty is aware of exposure, there is continued hazard of spreading the agent to other body surfaces. Therefore, until effective decontamination is performed, medical personnel who are handling a victim are at risk of becoming casualties themselves. Factors that shorten the duration of the latent period include increased intensity of exposure and increased temperature and humidity. Site of exposure and variation in individual susceptibility affect latency as well, which may range from 1 hr to more than 24 hr. Individuals previously exposed to mustard gas experience shorter latency and more severe injury on repeat exposure.

CLINICAL MANIFESTATIONS

Cutaneous Injury

The latency of onset and severity of skin injury after sulfur mustard exposure in healthy adult men varies based on the type of exposure and the tissue areas exposed. Liquid droplet exposures produce a deeper, more severe blister than that caused by absorption of the same amount of vapor over a wider area. Thinner skin, such as on the neck, axillae, and groin, is much more severely affected than skin of the palms and soles. The sensitivity of the groin and the need for elimination, even when wearing protective clothing, makes mustard injury in that area especially likely. As a result, fear of injury to the genital region could lead to voluntary postponement of urination and defecation, potentially resulting in urinary infections and fecal impaction. Preventive use of a topical skin protectant could lessen such concerns. The vapor exposure that would be expected to cause incapacitating skin blisters in half of a patient sample (ICT_{50}) is 1,000 to 2,000 mg-min/m^3, expressed as the product of vapor concentration and exposure time for whole body exposures. This is an area concentration that can easily be reached in the target area of a single mustard-filled aerial bomb or several artillery shells.

Once the skin is exposed, blisters develop after a period of itching and erythema, with the basal epidermal cell as the key cellular target of sulfur mustard in skin. By light microscopy, nuclear swelling begins within 3 to 9 hr after exposure, followed by nuclear pyknosis and vacuolation of cytoplasm. Edema at the epidermal–dermal junction is seen within 12 hr of exposure, and by 16 hr there is separation, with formation of coalescing vesicles. Blisters break and denude during the first week after exposure, and new blisters may form near others that are well developed.

Ocular Injury

In the conjunctiva and cornea, sulfur mustard exposure causes loosening of epithelial cells accompanied by corneal edema and opacification (Warthin & Weller, 1919). Even low-dose exposure of sulfur mustard to the eyes can be incapacitating (ocular ICt_{50} = 50 to 100 mg-min/m^3). Only limited studies of sulfur mustard-induced eye injuries in animals are available (Kadar et al., 1996; Maumenee & Scholz, 1948; Warthin & Weller, 1919). These suggest that the microscopic pathology is similar to most chemical injuries with the exception of acid and alkali burns.

In the conjunctiva, sulfur mustard exposure results in rapid vasodilation, increased vascular permeability, and edema. Mucus secretion is noticeable within 30 min. The primary medical care principles for ocular exposure consist of irrigation followed by prevention of infections and scarring. Casualties with more severe injuries receive topical antibiotics and topical mydriatics, such as atropine, to keep the pupils dilated. In addition, petroleum jelly is applied to the eyelids to prevent them from adhering to each other (Sidell et al., 1997). Reviews of battlefield mustard gas exposure stress the potential for relatively rapid visual incapacitation of large numbers of individuals (Vedder, 1925; Warthin, Weller, & Herrmann, 1918). One can envision that even mild eye irritation in large numbers of individuals will significantly reduce unit operational effectiveness. Approximately 90% of people with eye injury are visually disabled for approximately 10 days with conjunctivitis, photophobia, and minimal corneal swelling. The remaining 10% of victims with significant corneal involvement are at risk for corneal ulceration but rarely for anterior chamber scarring and neovascularization, any of which would result in prolonged disability. As fear of permanent blindness can lead to severe depression (Alexander, 1947), it may be critical for medical personnel to interdict at this point with reassurances about long-term recovery. Any treatments that can diminish discomfort and restore a modicum of vision to allow self-care and navigation would offer the patient major psychological benefits. In the most severely affected ocular injuries, recurrent corneal ulcerative disease has occurred 15 to 20 years after exposure (Pechura & Rall, 1993). A recent review of the toxicology and treatment of human ocular injury was published by Solberg, Alcalay, and Belkin (1997).

Respiratory Tract Injury

Although incapacitating airway injury occurs at vapor exposures significantly lower than those that cause severe skin blistering, inhaled sulfur mustard injures respiratory epithelium from the nasopharynx to the bronchioles. Since WWI, the majority of deaths occurring in sulfur mustard casualties have resulted from respiratory complications (Vedder, 1925; Warthin et al., 1918; Willems, 1989). Mild cases are treated to allow maximum comfort, whereas severe cases must attain adequate oxygenation. Because of the multiple ways respiratory injury can be expressed, treatment options vary with the patient (Sidell et al., 1997). In this regard, an inhaled vapor exposure in the range of 1,000 mg-min/m^3 is estimated to be lethal for half of those exposed, whereas the respiratory incapacitating dose is estimated to be in the range of 150 to 600 mg-min/m^3. One third of the Iranian casualties, when monitored 2 years after exposure, demonstrated chronic respiratory disease (Balali-Mood, 1996).

Systemic Toxicity and Chronic Effects

In general, a battlefield chemical casualty has also responded intensely to other stresses, such as sleep and food deprivation, dehydration, thermal extremes, and the summation of exposure to multiple blasts, concussions, and inhalation of smoke and combustion products. Reports of wartime sulfur mustard casualties show considerable variation in the occurrence of such findings as prostration, circulatory collapse, impaired cognition, severe headache, nausea and vomiting, lethargy, and depression (Vedder, 1925; Warthin et al., 1918; Willems, 1989). The extent of this variation suggests that factors other than sulfur mustard exposure may contribute to these problems.

Suppression of leukocyte production is common in severely ill sulfur mustard casualties (Stewart, 1918; Willems, 1989). Of 65 Iran–Iraq War (1979–1980) casualties evaluated in European hospitals, 29 had leukopenia to some degree (Willems, 1989). Although these severely injured patients were a subset of all casualties, this information suggests that there is sufficient systemic absorption of sulfur mustard after heavy battlefield exposure to pose a risk of carcinogenesis similar to that seen for biologically equivalent doses of alkylating compounds used in tumor chemotherapy. Sulfur mustard has been shown to have mutagenic (Cappizzi, Smith, Field, & Papirmeister, 1973), teratogenic (Rozmiarek, Cappizzi, Papirmeister, Furman, & Smith, 1973), and carcinogenic (Watson, Jones, & Griffin, 1989) potential. In studies of factory workers exposed to low levels of sulfur mustard for prolonged periods of time, increased incidences of lung, pharyngeal, and laryngeal cancers have been documented (Easton, Peto, & Doll, 1988).

The reported proportion of casualties who fully recover from sulfur mustard respiratory injury varies from over 90% (Vedder, 1925) to only 20% (Balali-Mood, 1986). Much of this variation can be explained by differences among patients and by attribution of chronic bronchitic symptoms to previous mustard gas exposure in the presence of ongoing causes such as heavy smoking. Major chronic problems such as bronchiectasis and recurrent pneumonia appear confined to casualties who had severe pulmonary infections complicating the acute injury (Urbanetti, 1988). Ocular and skin injuries generally heal completely but with the need for corneal transplantation or for skin grafting to deal with uncommon complications.

Central nervous system and cardiac anomalies have only been seen after extremely high doses of sulfur mustard and usually only in laboratory settings with animal models. Mustard gas casualties from the Iran–Iraq War (1979–1980) treated in Europe did not display severe central nervous system or cardiac abnormalities (Willems, 1989). On the other hand, persistent damage to the afferent nerve system was a common finding in patients suffering cutaneous mustard injuries (Thomsen, Eriksen, & Smit-Nielsen, 1998).

PSYCHOLOGICAL ASPECTS OF MUSTARD EXPOSURE

Neuropsychiatric symptoms such as depression and anxiety can be observed in victims after mustard exposure and, in general, can be attributed to characteristics of posttraumatic stress disorder (PTSD; Balali-Mood, 1996; Pechura & Rall, 1993). In a study of 535 Iranian patients exposed to mustard attack in the Iran–Iraq War, 12% demonstrated psychiatric problems, including agitation, depression, insomnia, and muscle weakness (Momeni, Enshaeih, Meghdadi, & Amindjavaheri, 1992). In a different study, all of 10 Iranian patients treated in Germany within 4 to 6 days following mustard exposure exhibited somnolence and apathy, with 1 individual presenting symptoms of psychosis. These symptoms subsided within a week, but unfortunately, no long-term follow-up studies were obtained (Eisenmenger, Drasch, Von Clarmann, Kretschmer, & Roider, 1991).

In one report from WWI, however, severe apathy and general indifference were observed as chronic consequences of large acute exposure to sulfur mustard (Henlly, 1956). Specific neurological disorders, such as impaired concentration, diminished libido, and sensory hypersensitivity, were also demonstrated in workers from chemical warfare plants, but these workers were exposed to other agents besides sulfur mustard (Lohs, 1975).

Fifty years after controlled mustard exposures, Schnurr, Green, and Friedman (1996) studied a cohort of 24 men who had taken part in the U.S. military's mustard gas testing program during WWII. Although the sample did not allow the investigators to generalize their findings on the prevalence of psychiatric disorders among surviving participants, they were able to conclude that "some men have PTSD due to their participation in the WWII mustard gas tests."

In their review of the psychological aspects of threats of chemical warfare including mustard gas, Stokes and Banderet (1997) pointed out that there are many stress-producing features of these agents: Most people are unfamiliar with chemical threat agents, the agents are insidious in their nature, many of the agents are persistent and can spread from their original target area, false alarms are easily generated, and many of these agents attack one of our most basic needs to survive—the ability to breathe.

DEVELOPMENT OF MEDICAL COUNTERMEASURES

After the discovery at the end of WWII that Germany had manufactured nerve agents, medical chemical defense research focused largely on protection against these compounds. The recent Iran–Iraq War (1980s) stimulated a renewed concern about the dangers of sulfur mustard. Fortunately, much of our knowledge about other alkylating compounds used in oncology has been helpful in intensifying efforts directed at preventing or minimizing sulfur mustard vesicating injury.

For example, Papirmeister, Gross, Meier, Petrali, and Johnson (1985) proposed a hypothesis to link alkylation of DNA with the cellular events of blister formation. According to their proposal, alkylation of DNA by sulfur mustard results in strand breaks that trigger activation of a nuclear DNA repair enzyme, poly(ADP-ribose) polymerase (PARP). Excessive activity of this enzyme depletes cellular stores of NAD+, a critical energy transfer substrate that is also needed for glycolysis (Gross, Meier, Papirmeister, Brinkley, & Johnson, 1985; Meier, Gross, & Papirmeister, 1987; Mol, Van de Ruit, & Kluivers, 1989). Inhibition of glycolysis (Dixon & Needham, 1946) causes a build up of glucose-6-phosphate, which serves as a substrate in the hexose monophosphate shunt. In turn, stimulation of the hexose monophosphate shunt results in activation of cellular proteases (Schnyder & Bagglionoi, 1980). These proteases could account for the cleavage of the adherent fibrils connecting the basal epidermal cell layer to the basement membrane.

Studies at the U.S. Army Medical Research Institute of Chemical Defense are thus far consistent with the proposal that, with the exception of activation of hexose monophosphate shunt (Martens, 1994), this biochemical cascade may contribute to blister formation. In addition, however, the process would appear to require an active inflammatory response and altered fluid dynamics in the affected tissue to generate the very large blisters seen after sulfur mustard exposure.

In the late 1980s and early 1990s, the U.S. Army's Medical Research and Materiel Command focused its research efforts on sulfur mustard to develop medical countermeasures that could ameliorate or eliminate the injury produced by exposure to mustard. Based on research from many sources, we have been able to derive a schematic representation of the major events involved in the mustard injury (Figure 1) and have been able to select from these events six areas of pharmacological intervention into the injury process (Table 1). For each of these six areas, we have identified at least one compound showing efficacy in in vitro or in vivo models of mustard toxicity. The results of this drug discovery program were summarized at the 22nd Army Science conference (W. J. Smith, Babin, Kiser, & Casillas, 2000). The results of this research effort and related medical chemical defense programs will be the generation of tangible benefits to the members of the U.S. armed forces. Specific drugs to protect against vesicant agents, treatments that reduce the

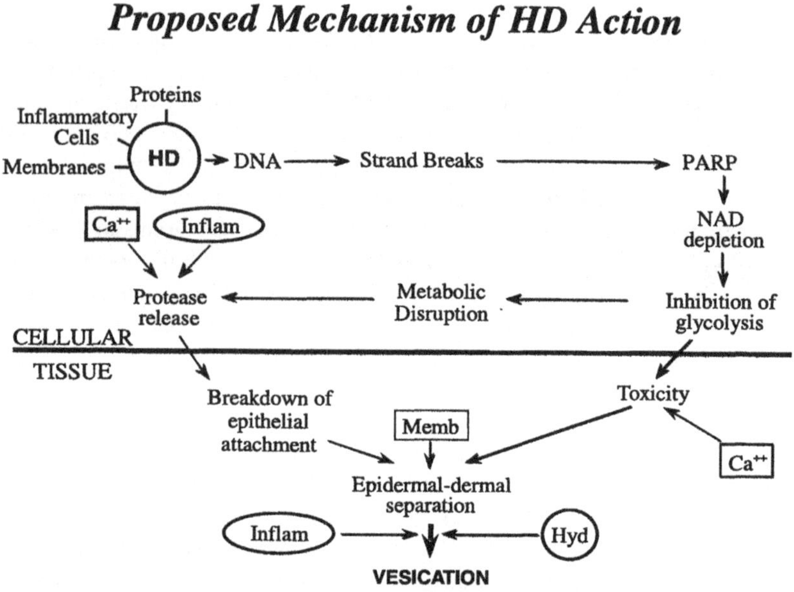

FIGURE 1 Cellular and tissue alterations induced by HD that are proposed to result in blister formation. HD can have many direct effects, such as alkylation of proteins and membrane components (Memb), as well as activation of inflammatory cells. One of the main macromolecular targets is DNA, with subsequent activation of poly(ADP-ribose) polymerase (PARP). Activation of PARP can initiate a series of metabolic changes culminating in protease activation. Within the tissue, the penultimate event is the epidermal–dermal separation that occurs in the lamina lucida of the basement membrane zone. Accompanied by a major inflammatory response and changes in the tissue hydrodynamics (Hyd), fluid fills the cavity formed at this cleavage plane and presents as a blister.

TABLE 1
Strategies for Pharmacological Intervention

Biochemistry	*Strategy*	*Example*
DNA alkylation	Intracellular scavengers	N-acetyl-L-cysteine
DNA strand breaks	Cell cycle inhibitors	Mimosine
PARP activation	PARP inhibitors	Niacinamide
Disruption of Ca^{++}	Calcium modulators	BAPTA (Ca^{++} chelator)
Protease activation	Protease inhibitors	Sulfonyl fluorides
Inflammation	Anti-inflammatories	Indomethacin

healing time, and reduction of performance decrements due to blister formation are just a few of the medical advances expected over the next few years.

Until definitive medical therapeutics for sulfur mustard are fielded, the medical caregivers will have to rely on symptomatic treatments and sound medical judgments. Historically derived treatments, as presented in the *Textbook of Military Medicine* (Sidell et al., 1997) and the *Medical Management of Chemical Casualties Handbook* (1999) prepared by the Chemical Casualty Care Division of the U.S. Army Medical Research Institute of Chemical Defense, can also be of assistance.

MEANS TO REDUCE PSYCHOLOGICAL STRESS

Until countermeasures are fielded to ameliorate or eliminate mustard gas injury, it is necessary to provide the warfighter with physical protection in the form of chemical protective clothing (for information on the effects of chemical protective clothing on military performance, see Krueger & Banderet, 1997) and equipment and the best possible medical casualty management. Although protective garments provided to the armed forces are effective, there are always potential problems with comfort and dexterity and adherence to timely use. Furthermore, a risk of exposure exists at garment openings and for those individuals who, because of their jobs, cannot wear full protective gear. To that end, the U.S. Army is developing a cream to enhance the protective capacity of currently worn field clothing (K. J. Smith, Hurst, Moeller, Skelton, & Sidell, 1995).

Knowledge gained from WWI casualties, accidental exposures, and victims of mustard gas attacks during the Iran–Iraq War has enabled the U.S. Army Medical Research Institute of Chemical Defense to provide medical practitioners with the latest information on medical management of chemical casualties. In evaluating patients, medical casualties of sulfur mustard will fall into one of three categories: return to duty, non-life-threatening but not return to duty, or life-threatening injuries (Sidell et al., 1997). Patients who can return to duty present small areas of erythema or blisters in noncritical areas of the skin, eye irritation, or late-onset, mild respiratory symptoms such as hoarseness or throat irritation and cough. If medical evaluation suggests the symptoms will not worsen, the patients can be given symptomatic therapy and returned to duty. Symptomatic treatment must include thorough, informed, credible explanations of treatment; expectations for immediate and long-term prognosis; and full documentation of the service member's medical records. Failure in any of these steps could result in severe, negative, long-term consequences. The other two more serious categories will require intense medical care (Moore & Keeler, 1993; Sidell et al., 1997). Whereas eye care and airway care will promote healing in these areas within weeks, skin injuries may require extended hospitalizations. It is encouraging to note that most Iranian patients treated in Europe were able to return home in fairly good condition within 10 weeks of treatment (Willems, 1989). However, from the standpoint of military performance or unit readiness, this constitutes a devastating injury.

Of course, a fourth category of mustard gas casualty can emerge—the conditions variously know as "gas neurosis" or "gas mania," that is, soldiers who believe they have been exposed to chemical agents and have symptoms, but in whom no physical evidence of exposure can be detected (for an extensive review of these historical war phenomena, see Stokes & Banderet, 1997). Besides these medical cases, one must be aware that in every conflict there are the shirkers (Heller, 1984): individuals who feign being exposed or deliberately expose themselves to contaminated material in order to be evacuated.

As for the six proposed medical countermeasures presented in Table 1 (intracellular scavengers, DNA cell cycle modulators, PARP inhibitors, calcium modulators, antiproteases, and anti-inflammatories), there is no evidence, at this time, that acute prophylactic or therapeutic usage of any of these six strategies will generate performance decrements in the warfighter. However, no systematic animal or human studies have been undertaken to address such problems. Although it is recognized that therapy with steroids or nonsteroidal anti-inflammatories can be accompanied by psychological side effects (Hoppmann, Peden, & Ober, 1991; Kaufmann, Kahaner, Peselow, & Gershon, 1982), the patient who experiences these symptoms will already be under extensive medical care, and aberrant responses to the therapy can be managed.

Overcoming the stress produced in a chemically threatening environment requires information on the nature of the threat and confidence that every possible step has been taken to eliminate or minimize the threat. Correct use of a gas mask can eliminate a great portion of the mustard gas injury by eradicating ocular and respiratory injuries. Proper use of sensors and military intelligence will reduce the risk of exposure and, therefore, of stress.

Training with these defensive measures can improve the warfighter's confidence in their effectiveness. Furthermore, frequent and extensive training with chemical defensive measures can also counteract the biggest problem with nuclear, biological, and chemical threats (i.e., the tendency to overestimate risks associated with unfamiliar and ambiguous threats; Stokes & Banderet, 1997). Knowing that the medical staff is prepared to deal with such injuries and can preserve life and minimize long-term consequences of injury can reduce the impact of the unfamiliar. In fact, inclusion of cognitive behavioral training as part of combat preparedness might transform a soldier's self-perception from that of an "aggrieved and helpless victim to a self-perception of resilient and adaptive survivor" (Stokes & Banderet, 1997, p. 405). Battlefield troops will always be subject to PTSD, but efforts under the U.S. Army Medical Research and Materiel Command are aimed at minimizing or eliminating the psychological and medical consequences of the vesicant agent threats.

ACKNOWLEDGMENTS

The opinions contained herein are the private views of the author and are not to be construed as official or as reflecting the views of the Army or the Department of Defense.

REFERENCES

Alexander, S. F. (1947). Medical report of the Bari Harbor mustard casualties. *The Military Surgeon, 101,* 1–17.

Balali-Mood, M. (1986). First reports of delayed toxic effects of yperite poisoning in Iranian fighters. In B. Heyndricks (Ed.), *Terrorism: Analysis and detection of explosives* (pp. 489–495). Ghent, Belgium: Rijksuniversiteit.

Balali-Mood, M. (1996). Delayed toxic effects of sulfur mustard in 1428 patients. In *Proceedings of the Chemical Biological Medical Treatment Symposium: An exploration of present capabilities and future requirements* (pp. 125–133). Spiez, Switzerland.

Cappizzi, R. L., Smith, W. J., Field, R. J., & Papirmeister, B. (1973). A host-mediated assay for chemical mutagens using the L5178Y/Asn(-) murine leukemia. *Mutation Research, 21,* 6.

Carus, W. S. (1988). *Chemical weapons in the Middle East* (Res. Memo No. 9:1–15). Washington, DC: Washington Institute for Near East Policy, Policy Focus.

Dixon, M., & Needham, D. M. (1946). Biochemical research on chemical warfare agents. *Nature, 158,* 512–518.

Easton, D. F., Peto, J., & Doll, R. (1988). Cancers of the respiratory tract in mustard gas workers. *British Journal of Industrial Medicine, 45,* 653–659.

Eisenmenger, W., Drasch, G., Von Clarmann, M., Kretschmer, E., & Roider, G. (1991). Clinical and morphological findings on mustard gas [bis(2-chloroethyl)sulfide] poisoning. *Journal of Forensic Sciences, 36,* 1688–1698.

Gross, C. L., Meier, H. L., Papirmeister, B., Brinkley, F. B., & Johnson, J. B. (1985). Sulfur mustard lowers nicotinamide dinucleotide concentrations in human skin grafted to athymic nude mice. *Toxicology & Applied Pharmacology, 81,* 85–90.

Hay, A., & Robert, G. (1990). The use of poison gas against the Iraqi Kurds: Analysis of bomb fragments, soil, and wool samples [Letter to the editor]. *Journal of the American Medical Association, 263,* 1065–1066.

Heller, C. E. (1984). *Chemical warfare in World War I: The American experience, 1917–1918* (Leavenworth Papers No. 10). Fort Leavenworth, KS: Combat Studies Institute, Command and General Staff College.

Henlly, F. (1956). Mass intoxication due to explosion of shell containing dichloroethyl sulfide dating back to World War I. *Annales de Medicine Legale, 36,* 195–204.

Hoppmann, R. A., Peden, J. G., & Ober, S. K. (1991). Central nervous system side effects of non-steroidal anti-inflammatory drugs. *Archives of Internal Medicine, 151,* 1309–1313.

Hu, H., Cook-Deegan, R., & Shurki, A. (1989). The use of chemical weapons: Mounting an investigation using survey epidemiology. *Journal of the American Medical Association, 262,* 640–651.

Kadar, T., Amir, A., Fishbeine, E., Chapman, S., Liani, H., Sahar, R., et al. (1996). The potential therapy of steroids against ocular lesions induced by sulfur mustard vapor in rabbits. In *Proceedings of the 1996 Medical Defense Bioscience Review* (pp. 845–852). Aberdeen Proving Ground, MD: U.S. Army Medical Research Institute of Chemical Defense.

Kaufmann, M., Kahaner, K., Peselow, E. D., & Gershon, S. (1982). Steroid psychoses: Case report and brief overview. *Journal of Clinical Psychiatry, 43,* 75–76.

Krueger, G. P., & Banderet, L. E. (Eds.). (1997). Effects of chemical protective clothing on military performance [Special issue]. *Military Psychology, 9*(4).

Lohs, K. (1975). *Delayed toxic effects of chemical warfare agents* (SIPRI monograph). Stockholm, Sweden: Almqvist & Wilksell.

Martens, M. E. (1994). Hexose monophosphate shunt activity in human epidermal keratinocytes exposed to sulfur mustard. In *Proceedings of the Meeting of Research Study Group-3 on Prophylaxis and Therapy Against Chemical Agents* (NATO Technical Proceedings AC/243(Panel 8)TP/9, pp. 6.1–6.4). Brussels, Belgium: NATO.

Maumenee, A. E., & Scholz, R. O. (1948). The histopathology of the ocular lesions produced by sulfur and nitrogen mustards. *Bulletin Johns Hopkins Hospital, 82,* 121–147.

Medical management of chemical casualties handbook (3rd ed.). (1999). Aberdeen Proving Ground, MD: U.S. Army Medical Research Institute of Chemical Defense, Chemical Casualty Care Office.

Meier, H. L., Gross, C. L., & Papirmeister, B. (1987). 2,2′-dichlorodiethyl sulfide (sulfur mustard) decreases NAD+ levels in human leukocytes. *Toxicology Letters, 39,* 109–122.

Mol, M. A. E., Van de Ruit, A. M. B. C., & Kluivers, A. W. (1989). NAD+ levels and glucose uptake of cultured human epidermal cells exposed to sulfur mustard. *Toxicology & Applied Pharmacology, 98,* 159–165.

Momeni, A., Enshaeih, S., Meghdadi, M., & Amindjavaheri, M. (1992). Skin manifestations of mustard gas. *Archives of Dermatology, 128,* 775–780.

Moore, D. W., & Keeler, J. R. (1993). Mustard agent poisoning: Pathophysiology and nursing implications. *Critical Care Nurse, 13,* 62–68.

Papirmeister, B., Feister, A. J., Robinson, S. I., & Ford, R. D. (1991). *Medical defense against mustard gas: Toxic mechanisms and pharmacological implications.* Boca Raton, FL: CRC Press.

Papirmeister, B., Gross, C. L., Meier, H. L., Petrali, J. P., & Johnson, J. B. (1985). Molecular basis for mustard-induced vesication. *Fundamental & Applied Toxicology, 5,* S134–S149.

Pechura, C. M., & Rall, D. P. (Eds.). (1993). *Veterans at risk: The health effects of mustard gas and lewisite.* Washington, DC: National Academy Press.

Rozmiarek, J., Cappizzi, R. L., Papirmeister, B., Furman, W. H., & Smith, W. J. (1973). Mutagenic activity in somatic and germ cells following chronic inhalation of sulfur mustard. *Mutation Research, 21,* 13.

Schnurr, P. P., Green, B. L., & Friedman, M. J. (1996). Post-traumatic stress disorder among World War II mustard gas test participants. *Military Medicine, 161,* 131–136.

Schnyder, J., & Bagglionoi, M. (1980). Induction of plasminogen activator secretion in macrophages by electrochemical stimulation of the hexose monophosphate shunt by methylene blue. *Proceedings of the National Academy of Science (USA), 77,* 414–417.

Sidell, F. R., Urbanetti, J. S., Smith, W. J., & Hurst, C. G. (1997). Vesicants. In R. Zajtchuk & R. F. Bellamy (Eds.), *Textbook of military medicine: Medical aspects of chemical and biological warfare* (pp. 197–228). Washington, DC: Office of the Surgeon General.

Smith, K. J., Hurst, C. G., Moeller, R. B., Skelton, H. G., & Sidell, F. R. (1995). Sulfur mustard: Its continuing threat as a chemical warfare agent, the cutaneous lesions induced, progress in understanding its mechanism of action, its long-term health effects, and new developments for protection and therapy. *Journal of the American Academy of Dermatology, 32,* 765–776.

Smith, W. J., & Dunn, M. A. (1991). Medical defense against blistering chemical warfare agents. *Archives of Dermatology, 127,* 1207–1213.

Smith, W. J., Babin, M. C., Kiser, R. C., & Casillas, R. P. (2000). Development of medical countermeasures to sulfur mustard vesication. In *Proceedings of the 22nd Army Science Conference* (pp. 314–318). Washington, DC: Assistant Secretary of the Army (Acquisition, Logistics & Technology).

Solberg, Y., Alcalay, M., & Belkin, M. (1997). Ocular injury by mustard gas. *Survey of Opthamology, 41,* 461–466.

Stewart, M. J. (1918). *Report on cases of poisoning by "mustard gas," with special reference to the histological changes and to alterations in the lymphocyte count* (Rep. No. 17). London: Chemical Warfare Medical Committee.

Stokes, J. W., & Banderet, L. E. (1997). Psychological aspects of chemical defense and warfare. *Military Psychology, 9,* 395–415.

Thomsen, A. B., Eriksen, J., & Smit-Nielsen, K. (1998). Chronic neuropathic symptoms after exposure to mustard gas: A long-term investigation. *Journal of the American Academy of Dermatology, 39,* 187–190.

United Nations. (1984, March). *Report of the specialists appointed by the Secretary-General to investigate allegations by the Islamic Republic of Iran concerning the use of chemical weapons* (Rep. No. S/16513). New York: Author.

United Nations. (1986, March). *Report of the mission dispatched by the Secretary-General to investigate allegations of the use of chemical weapons in the conflict between Iran and Iraq* (Rep. No. S/17911). New York: Author.

United Nations. (1987, May). *Report of the mission dispatched by the Secretary-General to investigate allegations of the use of chemical weapons in the conflict between the Islamic Republic of Iran and Iraq* (Rep. No. S/18852). New York: Author.

Urbanetti, J. S. (1988). Battlefield chemical inhalation injury. In J. Loke (Ed.), *Pathophysiology and treatment of inhalation injuries* (pp. 281–348). New York: Marcel Dekker.

Vedder, E. B. (1925). *The medical aspects of chemical warfare* (pp. 125–166). Baltimore: Williams & Wilkins.

Warthin, A. S., & Weller, C. V. (1919). *The medical aspects of mustard gas poisoning.* St. Louis: Mosby.

Warthin, A. S., Weller, C. V., & Herrmann, G. R. (1918). The ocular lesions produced by dichlorethylsulphide ("mustard gas"). *Journal of Laboratory & Clinical Medicine, 4,* 785–832.

Watson, A. P., Jones, T. D., & Griffin, G. D. (1989). Sulfur mustard as a carcinogen: Application of relative potency analysis to the chemical warfare agents H, HD, and HT. *Regulatory Toxicology & Pharmacology, 10,* 1–25.

Willems, J. L. (1989). Clinical management of mustard gas casualties. *Annales Medicinae Militaris Belgicae, 3*(Suppl.), 1–61.

MILITARY PSYCHOLOGY, 2002, *14*(2), 159–177

Neurotoxicological and Behavioral Effects of Cyanide and Its Potential Therapies

Steven I. Baskin
Pharmacology Division
U.S. Army Medical Research Institute of Chemical Defense
Aberdeen Proving Ground, Maryland

Gary A. Rockwood
Drug Assessment Division
U.S. Army Medical Research Institute of Chemical Defense
Aberdeen Proving Ground, Maryland

The use of the blood agent cyanide (CN) as a military threat agent has been recognized not only historically (Nero and Napoleon III) but also more currently in World War I, World War II, in the Iran–Iraq War in the 1980s, and elsewhere where terrorist activities have occurred. CN is easy and inexpensive to produce and can be obtained from normal commercial trade. CN can act very rapidly (within seconds) to prevent the normal utilization of oxygen by tissues. Excitable tissues, for example, heart and brain, are particularly affected. Hypoxia, convulsions, heart arrhythmias, and death can follow. If exposed, it is best to leave the affected area rapidly. Treatments such as nitrite, which forms methemoglobin that binds CN, and thiosulfate, which converts CN to thiocyanate, act within an appropriate time but produce central nervous system side effects. This article examines the literature on the neurotoxicological and behavioral effects of CN and its treatments. Sites and mechanisms of actions involved in these effects are evaluated. Factors that significantly alter the action of CN and may influence morbidity and mortality are discussed.

This article is part of a special issue, "Chemical Warfare and Chemical Terrorism: Psychological and Performance Outcomes," of *Military Psychology*, 2002, *14*(2), 83–177.

Requests for reprints should be sent to Steven I. Baskin, Pharmacology Division, U.S. Army Medical Research Institute of Chemical Defense, 3100 Ricketts Point Road, Aberdeen Proving Ground, MD 21010–5400.

Egyptians and Romans were known to use poisonous plant extracts as a method of suicide and murder. Preparations of cherry laurel water containing cyanogenic glycosides distilled from the bark of the tree were used by Romans, including Lacosta, who used such material to poison individuals who displeased Nero (Sollmann, 1948).

The blood agent cyanide (CN) had been proposed by Napoleon III to be placed on the tips of bayonets during the Franco–Prussian War and by Lord Playfair during the Crimean War. World War I (WWI) experiences taught that CN could produce rapid death in the field, but the WWI delivery systems did not allow for dependable application of the product (Macy, 1937). More efficient delivery systems and improved methods of synthesis and storage would later overcome problems encountered in WWI.

At the beginning of WWII, CN was used by the Japanese forces on the Bataan Peninsula in the form of a hand grenade and in Manchuria and China for poisoning wells (Williams & Wallace, 1989). The Nazis used the poison at the beginning of the war to eradicate entrenched Yugoslav partisans in caves and to kill over 2 million concentration camp inmates. In a final 3-day period, with the Russian forces approaching, Höss, the commandant of Auschwitz, increased the concentration of CN to accelerate the normal killing time for inmates of Zyklon B (hydrocyanic acid adsorbed onto a dispersible pharmaceutical base) to exterminate more than 10,000 Russian soldiers. In the 1980s, several Middle Eastern sites were reported to be CN targets: The inhabitants of Hama, Syria, were gassed (Lang, Mullin, Fenyvesi, Rosenberg, & Barnes, 1986), as were inhabitants of Halabja, Iraq, and possibly Shahabad, Iran, during the Iran–Iraq War in the 1980s (Heylin, 1988; "Medical Expert," 1985). Muslim terrorists in Turkey and Tajikistan used CN as a poison in the 1990s (Oehler, 1996). More recently, plans for use of CN as a terrorist weapon by Al-Qaeda have been made public (Follain & Rufford, 2001; Grey & Gadher, 2001).

Although CN can disperse rapidly at high temperatures, at lower temperatures CN provides stimulation of the chemoreceptors in the aortic arch activating a reflex respiratory gasp. It has been shown that it is not possible in the conscious human to prevent subsequent gasps following stimulation of the chemoreceptors. If the concentration of CN is sufficient, the subsequent inhalation of additional CN leads to unconsciousness, convulsion, and possibly death.

CN inhibits mitochondrial cytochrome oxidase in a number of organs, including the central nervous system (CNS), interfering with normal electron transfer. The mechanism of curtailing oxygen utilization in the brain is thought to produce unconsciousness and changes in certain behaviors. It is also believed that the interruption of oxygen utilization leads to convulsions, particularly in areas that employ electron transport. Ultimately, oxygen utilization is disrupted, and if untreated, CN-induced lethality results from hypoxia. It should be noted that the behavior and physiological effects of CN do not exactly mimic that of lack of oxygen. Interest in CN as a potential chemical warfare or terrorist agent is based on its limited but actual use in these capacities (Baskin & Brewer, 1997; Macy, 1937). Although of limited success on the battlefield in the past, CN is easy and relatively inexpensive to manufacture and is particularly lethal in small doses. Furthermore, its capacity for mass death in concentration camps during WWII add to the compelling reasons for continued military and civilian concern about CN.

Certain parameters of CN-induced lethality in man and other mammals have been examined for many years; however, because of its highly toxic and rapid-acting nature, much less is known about sublethal CN toxicity (D'Mello, 1987). It has been suggested that the CNS in general, and the brain in particular, are highly sensitive to the toxic effects of CN and may be the primary target system (Way, 1984; Way et al., 1984). Mangun and Skipper (1942) found, from observations during the execution of convicts, that a human is incapacitated (onset of convulsions) by approximately 10 mg/L in 10 to 18 sec. CNS changes due to non-CN-induced (e.g., hypoxic) hypoxia resemble that induced by CN, although the latter also produces enzyme and neurotransmitter changes (D'Mello, 1987). CN is generally considered a nonpersistent threat agent. However, within approximately 2 weeks of near lethal CN intoxication, delayed CNS behavioral effects and cerebellar or midbrain lesions have been noted in approximately 10% to 15% of mice, rats, or dogs (Haymaker, Ginzler, & Ferguson, 1952; Rose, Harris, & Chen, 1954). In humans, disruption of memory or attention deficit has been known to last up to a year (Macy, 1937). This was described by Barcroft (1931), who was a volunteer in a clinical CN experimental procedure.

SOURCES OF CYANIDE IN OUR ENVIRONMENT

There are many chemical forms of CN: organic CNs, nitriles, CN salts, hydrocyanic acid, and the anionic form. For the sake of discussion, the term CN refers in general to CN without reference to chemical form. However, where appropriate, chemical form is referenced (i.e., hydrogen cyanide, HCN; potassium cyanide, KCN; and sodium cyanide, NaCN).

CN is formed with every breath we take and exchanges at concentrations much less than what is considered toxic (Lundquist, Rosling, & Sorbo, 1988). Observations that animal life is constantly exchanging CN endogenously (e.g., Lundquist et al., 1988) and studies regarding its function as a central modulator in rats in its gaseous state similar to what has been seen for carbon monoxide (Borowitz, Gunasekar, & Isom, 1997) suggest that CN may provide a biological role as a neuromodulator in addition to that of an exogenous synthetic poison. Because the brain has been reported to be the organ most sensitive to CN (Way et al., 1984), some propose the CNS as a predominant site for the lethal effects of CN.

CN is found in many forms and precursors that can be taken into the body. It was noted from antiquity that ingestion of certain plants could result in a rapid reflex respiratory gasp followed by anoxia and convulsions, occasionally culminating in death. A wide variety of plant life incorporates nitrile-containing substances that are metabolically or chemically converted to CN and are toxic to both animals and humans (Evered, Robinson, & Rose, 1988). For example, a large number of plants in the Rosecea genus (e.g., cherry, peach, and bitter almond) are known to contain cyanogenic glycosides, and many of the behavioral and CNS effects of CN were originally observed after the ingestion of CN-containing plant products. Plants can contain cyanogenic lipids (e.g., in *Sapandous drummondii*) or cyanogenic glycosides (e.g., in cassava, sorghum, flax, and white clover). Cassava (*Manihot esculenta*) is a common crop used as a food (manioc) in parts of Asia, South America, and Africa, and if not properly processed, can pose a serious cyanogenic hazard. The plant stores a cyanogenic glycoside, linamarin, that is degraded by the enzyme linamarase to cyanohydrins and subsequently to hydrocyanic acid. Thus, it is probable that chronic ingestion of cyanogenic glycosides, particularly in an improperly washed product, could lead to behavioral changes that could be exacerbated in low-sulfur diets as well as by other factors.

Today, poisonings can result from contact with or by breathing silver-cleaning products, which contain CN. CN is also used in many industrial applications, such as electroplating, case-hardening steel manufacturing, mining, and agricultural fumigation. Products related to HCN by use of other nitriles include industrial solvents (e.g., acetonitrile [methylcyanide]) or nitrile polymers such as nylon that have become useful items in everyday life. However, these same products can, like nylon, depolymerize in fire and release short-chain monomers or CN, resulting in serious CNS toxicity or death.

THE BASIS OF CYANIDE INTOXICATION

CN is known to produce toxicological changes in many biological and chemical systems (Baskin & Brewer, 1997). Because the wide spectrum of hierarchical complexity of CN precludes a full review, this commentary is confined to the effects of CN on the central, and in some instances peripheral, nervous systems. Historically, the effects of CN were originally determined by in vitro metabolic studies (Warburg, 1925; Warburg, Negelein, & Haas, 1933). In addition, studies by Keilin (1929) showed the mechanism to be the inhibition of cytochrome oxidase in the mitochondria, reducing oxygen utilization by the tissue. Although CN can bind to both the oxidized and reduced forms of cytochrome oxidase, it possesses a greater affinity for the oxidized form (Van Buuren, Nicholls, & Van Gelder, 1972). In this manner, CN differs from carbon monoxide. Newer hypotheses have largely stressed different mechanisms based on in vivo models, as opposed to the more classical explanations that are based on in vitro models (Cassel, Karlsson, & Sellstrom, 1991; Cassel, Mjorndal, Persson, & Soderstrom, 1993; Cassel &

Persson, 1992). The convulsive effects of CN could also be dependent on changes in dopamine (Cassel, 1995; Cassel, Koch, & Tiger, 1995).

A growing number of papers suggest that CN-related CNS toxicity is not due to inhibition of cytochrome oxidase in the mitochondria but is due to a direct effect of CN on the glutamic acid receptors or to its interaction with cells of the CNS. Similarly, a body of research has investigated the interaction of CN with calcium and neuronal culture. Several other studies in isolated cerebellar granule neurons suggest that CN selectively augments kainate but not N-methyl-D-aspartate (NMDA)–induced release of glutamate and taurine (e.g., McCaslin & Yu, 1992), whereas another study observed effects on NMDA (Cai & McCaslin, 1992). Still further studies suggest that CN interacts with NMDA sites coupled to calcium (Patel, Peoples, Yim, & Isom, 1994; Patel, Yim, & Isom, 1993; Sun, Rane, Gunasekar, Borowitz, & Isom, 1999). Isolated receptor studies showed a specific subunit interaction of CN and the NMDA receptor (Arden, Sinor, Potthoff, & Aizenman, 1998). Several investigations were performed as in vitro experiments that used extremely large concentrations of CN (approximately 1 mM or more; Patel, Yim, & Isom, 1992), and some of the interactions of CN with glutamic acid occurred within approximately 0.5 to 1.0 hr. Because this is much longer than the time until death occurs from CN (1 to 3 min), the practical effects are in doubt. In addition, the time until unconsciousness takes place following CN exposure is approximately 15 to 30 sec, and the time until convulsions occur is 30 to 60 sec (HCN). The time to response for the alkaline salts of CN is longer. When comparing different species for sensitivity towards CN toxicity, it is noted that the order of the sensitivity of species can change as the route, concentration, or time of administration changes. These factors can influence the CNS toxicity as well as the estimate for CN in humans (McNamara, 1976).

CLINICAL SYMPTOMS OF CYANIDE INTOXICATION

CN is a rapidly acting poison in humans, with death occurring within minutes after inhalation or injection. Breathing CN in a concentration of 0.2 to 0.3 mg/L has been reported to kill almost immediately. However, inhaling a concentration of 0.13 mg/L can cause death in about 1 hr. Because the chemical form of CN influences the time course of absorption and distribution of CN, the onset of HCN toxicity, including CNS effects for example, is more rapid than for NaCN. CN has also been shown to be toxic at different doses and for different time onsets for different routes of exposure, which include intravenous, intramuscular, oral, application on normal or abraded skin, or ocular administration (Ballantyne, 1987). Factors such as first-pass effect and enterohepatic circulation can result in prolonged toxicity. Age and state of health as well as the mode of ingestion and the chemical form of CN will additionally have a great effect on the chemical's toxicity. Other factors, such as the ingestion of cyanogenic foods like almonds, cassava, lima beans, and other lentils, as well as smoking, may increase endogenous levels of CN in the body. Even diseases, such as multiple sclerosis, may elevate blood CN levels (Fowler & Durbetaki, 1952). In CN poisoning, the oxygen content of venous blood becomes similar or even higher than that of arterial blood (Johnson & Mellors, 1988), and the venous blood can appear bright red. As a result, lactic acid accumulates, and a metabolic acidosis can develop.

Further complicating diagnosis and treatment, the clinical signs and symptoms of CN poisoning may change very rapidly. CNS abnormalities range from headache and dizziness or unconsciousness, or both, to seizures, coma, and death. Early symptoms can also include tachycardia, pain in the cardiac region, muscular weakness, speech difficulty, intense salivation, nausea, bitter sense of taste with numbness, dullness of the tongue and mouth, and fever. F. M. Vincent (1986) and M. Vincent, Vincent, Marka, and Faure (1981) showed that neuronal neuritis (optic neuritises or sciatica) from CN exposure appears to correlate with increased CN concentrations in the blood and urine. Seizures develop as a result of hypoxia rather than CNS stimulation. At this time, loss of movement, poor coordination, and drowsiness occur. In cats and nonhuman primates, doses of 0.5 to 1.2 mg/kg of NaCN can produce "convulsions" (a decerebrate state) due to actions of CN on the facilitatory region in the pontine tegmentum; humans are thought to be similarly affected (Lipton, 1947).

In death from CN, the oxygen-saturated blood can sometimes give the skin a reddish color, and uncontrolled urination and defecation may occur. The blood remains fluid for a long time, and postmortem changes show a slow development of decay. There is also a continuous drainage in the mucous membrane of the heart and pleura. In peroral poisoning due to metallic salts of CN, there can be damage to the mucous membrane because of release of a caustic base (Radonjic, Boskovic, & Pribic, 1983). In the nonhuman primate, the delayed death from CN produced pathologic changes that occurred largely in the cerebellum (Coon, Glass, Sonkin, & Luahbaugh, 1943). In an attempted-suicide patient, the basal ganglia (putamen), as measured by computer tomography and magnetic resonance imaging before death and globus pallidus at death, were highly sensitive to the effects of CN (Messing & Storch, 1988). The primary hypoxic effect in the CNS in nonhuman primates and rodents appeared in the white matter, with necrosis occurring more frequently than nerve demyelination (Hurst, 1940; Way, 1981). Studies by Ferguson, Ginzler, Bodansky, Boyers, and Jandorff (1945) found that a sublethal dose appeared to result in irreversible injury to susceptible nervous tissue, and foci of hemorrhage and necrosis were described within both the cortical and medullary areas of the cerebrum and cerebellum. In the cerebellum, there were also degenerative changes of many Purkinje cells, and glial and capillary proliferation was found in the cerebellum and within the cerebrum. In addition to hemorrhage and necrosis, there were degenerative lesions of Nissl bodies of neurons, especially the large pyramidal and

Betz cells. Perifocal inflammatory reaction gliosis, accumulations of fat-laden gitter cells, and capillary proliferation were also observed in individual animals.

The respiratory symptoms occur over two phases. In the first phase, hypoxic stimulation of chemoreceptors and the central respiratory center results in tachypnea and dyspnea. In the second phase, the respiratory rate slows and usually progresses to apnea. This progression is rapid and is probably the result of a hypoxic effect on the respiratory center in the medulla (Holland & Kozlowski, 1986).

PROGNOSIS

The fate of the subject is usually decided within the first half hour after ingestion and depends on the quantity of poison absorbed and the length of time between the poisoning and the beginning of therapy. In about 20% of dogs, a delayed death may occur in which brain lesions are noted (Haymaker et al., 1952). This is frequently observed in higher animals and probably in humans due to complications arising from the acute neural anoxia (Coon et al., 1943).

INTERACTIONS OF CYANIDE WITH CARBON MONOXIDE AND OTHER LIGANDS

The CNS toxicity of CN is additive with that of carbon monoxide (CO; Levin, Paabo, Gurman, Clark, & Yoklavich, 1988). Although requiring unique conditions, CN and CO can each produce lactic acidosis of the type that can cause circulatory insufficiency (Orii, 1985; Piantadosi & Sylvia, 1984). CN and CO also appear to exert an additive effect on certain behaviors.

Thiosulfate shows poor pharmacokinetics and absorption and can cause vomiting as well as temporary hypertension (Baskin, Horowitz, & Nealley, 1992; Radonjic et al., 1983). Hyperbaric oxygen has also been used apparently successfully for low-level CN intoxication in the presence of thiosulfate and methemoglobin formers (Trapp, 1970). In addition, cobalt salts have been effective CN antidotes. However, the delayed toxicity, including depression of breathing and heart function as well as convulsion, makes this class of compounds less desirable. Chronic administration of methemoglobin-forming compounds that form low amounts of methemoglobin can still produce functional changes in the CNS. Weger (1969) found that a therapeutic dose of 4-DMAP (a methemoglobin former), for example, produced an immediate and continuous increase in blood flow to the brain. This phenomenon also occurred in a brain that had been damaged by the reduced blood flow after CN poisoning (Paulet, 1955). Ten percent and even 5% prolonged methemoglobin in the blood can produce an effect more pronounced than a transient presence of the same concentration (Garbuz, 1971).

CYANIDE AND BEHAVIOR

McMahon and Birnbaum (1990) suggested that "it is the disposition of CN within the brain that may be most important in assessing the acute toxicity of the compound" (p. 313). The following discussion describes available information on the sublethal effects of CN on behavior and related parameters, as well as the behavioral effects of CN treatments and prophylactics.

Dietary Cyanide Exposure

The effects of sublethal CN on behavior and function largely reflect CNS changes. In addition to data from accidental (industrial exposure) or intentional (attempted or successful acts of suicide) CN exposure (Vogel, Sultan, & Ten Eyck, 1981), certain foods (such as cassava root and certain beans) that are staples in different parts of the world also contain varying levels of CN. The amount of CN in these foods is usually below lethal levels (but see Aregheore & Agunbiade, 1991); however, if consumed in sufficient quantity over time, CN can accumulate within the body. Cassava root, which contains high levels of cyanogenic glycosides, is a high-yield crop in poor quality soil, making it attractive as a basic source of nutrition in certain regions of Africa, including Mozambique, Tanzania, and Zaire (Howlett, Brubaker, Mlingi, & Rosling, 1990). When cassava is processed properly (e.g., soaked for 3 to 5 days), CN content can be reduced effectively (Tylleskär et al., 1991). However, if processing is inadequate (e.g., soaked for less than 3 days), CN removal is incomplete and consumption may be dangerous.

Ingestion of inadequately processed cassava can, over time, result in neurological dysfunction. A specific neurological disorder similar to paralysis, Konzo is reported among people whose regular diets contain cassava and related cyanogenic-containing substances. Konzo is a permanent but nonprogressive spastic paraparesis (muscle weakness) that has been studied extensively by Rosling and colleagues (Howlett et al., 1990; Tylleskär et al., 1995). This disease also causes high urinary and serum levels of thiocyanate. In addition, low urinary inorganic sulfate is indicative of a low intake of sulfur and is consistent with low protein-rich foods. Low intake of dietary sulfur can exacerbate sensitivity to CN and CN-like compounds.

These and related studies suggest that chronic CN intake can contribute to medical conditions indicative of chronic persistent CN intoxication. Howlett et al. (1990) described the typical developmental course of Konzo as beginning with generalized weakness, difficulty in walking, and trembling. Eventually, affected individuals tend to fall while walking and soon lose their ability to stand or walk. Lower back pain and lower limb numbness have also been described (Howlett et al., 1990).

Experimental Models

In addition to problems associated with ingestion of foods containing low levels of CN, various manufacturing procedures (e.g., electroplating) involve the use of CN or CN-like products or by-products. Because the CNS is highly sensitive to CN, an understanding of chronic, low-level exposure, particularly on the CNS, is clearly warranted. Several behavioral models have been established to further characterize sublethal CN toxicity. Although lethality is observed only minutes after exposure to a sufficient amount of CN, significant behavioral and functional alterations following exposure to sublethal doses of CN have also been observed. In addition, CN pretreatments and postexposure treatments can also affect behavior.

Motor function. In addition to motor impairment in humans who are exposed chronically to low levels of CN (e.g., Konzo), Parkinson-like effects have also been observed in humans exposed to CN (Rosenow, Herholz, Lanfermann, Weuthen, & Heiss, 1995). To elucidate the mechanisms and to further characterize this type of impairment, animal studies have been conducted on the effects of sublethal CN on motor function.

In a study designed to examine the neurochemical, histological, and locomotor effects of CN on dopaminergic function in mice, Kanthasamy, Borowitz, Pavlakovic, and Isom (1994) injected animals subcutaneously (SC) with a sublethal dose of KCN, 6.0 mg/kg, twice daily across 7 days. Another treatment group received only a single 6.0 mg/kg KCN SC injection. Control animals received SC injections of saline and were either fed ad lib or pair-fed with the appropriate KCN-treated animals. Functional endpoints evaluated included locomotor activity (90 min in an activity cage), experimental catalepsy (latency to remove forepaws from a 2.5-cm block), and experimental akinesia (latency to move all four paws). All motor measurements were made following the final KCN administration. Compared with controls, motor impairment (i.e., hypoactivity and increased latency in the catalepsy and akinesia tests) was observed in the multidosed but not the singly dosed KCN-treated animals. However, in the singly dosed animals, muscle weakness and respiratory depression were observed during the first 15-min post-KCN exposure. Others have reported muscle weakness following CN in rodents (Ashton, Van Reempts, & Wauquier, 1981) as well as in dogs (Marrs, Bright, & Swanson, 1982).

Locomotor activity and akinesia effects in the multidosed animals were, at least in part, a reflection of KCN-induced dopaminergic depletion, because each corresponded with decreased striatal dopamine activity (see also Persson, Cassel, & Sellström, 1985). Furthermore, the addition of l-DOPA reversed these effects on performance. Interestingly, l-DOPA therapy has also successfully mitigated Parkinson-like symptoms in CN-exposed humans (Rosenow et al., 1995; Uitti, Rajput, Ashenhurst, & Rozdilsky, 1985).

Kanthasamy et al. (1994) also performed neurochemical as well as histological evaluations as a function of KCN exposure. Compared with controls, reduced dopamine levels were observed in the striatum and hippocampus, and fewer dopamine neurons were detected in the basal ganglia of KCN-treated animals. These findings are important in the context of the observed motor impairment, because toxicant-induced basal ganglia disruption has been associated with locomotor deficits (Langston, Ballard, Terrud, & Irwin, 1983).

Mills, Gunasekar, Li, Borowitz, and Isom (1999) further characterized brain regions selectively affected by chronic administration of KCN to mice. The parietal and suprarhinal regions of the motor cortex showed DNA fragmentation, whereas vacuolization, cell loss, and gliosis (but not DNA fragmentation) were observed in the substantia nigra. Interestingly, the distinct regions of brain damage appear to be due to differing modes of cell death.

In a report on the sublethal CN effects in guinea pigs, D'Mello (1985, 1987) included a description of CN-induced swimming deficits. Animals were placed in a swim tank, required to turn around 180° and then swim to an escape platform. Compared with solvent-treated controls, animals treated SC with NaCN (2.0 or 4.0 mg/kg) displayed an increased time to start swimming, an increased time to complete swimming, and fewer spontaneous turns. This swim latency was affected by a dose of CN as low as 1.75 mg/kg and performance impairment peaked at 8 to 16 min after NaCN injection. Administering the anti-CN methemoglobin former p-aminopropiophenone (PAPP; 25 mg/kg) 15 min prior to NaCN exposure greatly reduced NaCN behavioral toxicity. Increasing the time between PAPP and NaCN reduced the capacity of PAPP to protect against this impairment.

Learning

Active avoidance. D'Mello (1987) administered NaCN (0.0, 1.0, 2.0, or 3.0 mg/kg) SC to guinea pigs well trained on an active avoidance task, in which animals were required to cross from one side of a test chamber to the other to escape from or avoid an electric current applied to the grid floor. A trained animal will learn that these cues allow for anticipation of current onset as evidenced by a shift from escape behavior to avoidance behavior during training. At 2.0 and 3.0 mg/kg, NaCN decreased the number of avoidance responses and increased the number of escape responses, response latency, and response time. It is not likely that these observations were related to a motor deficit because the number of intertrial crossings was not affected.

Morris water maze. Intracerebroventricular (ICV) NaCN has been observed to disrupt normal spatial navigation in rats using the Morris water maze (MWM) swim task. In this task, rats were placed in a round water tank and trained to use spatial cues to locate an escape platform submerged just below the waterline.

Blokland, Bothmer, Honig, and Jolles (1993) reported that 5.0 μg, but not 2.5 μg, NaCN administered ICV significantly increased escape latency (time to locate and climb onto the escape platform) when administered 1 or 5 min prior to MWM testing. This was not evident when NaCN was administered 10 or 15 min prior to MWM testing. In a more recent study, 2.5 μg ICV NaCN was sufficient to produce some disruption on the MWM task, but results were inconsistent. However, as in the 1993 study, strong effects occurred on escape latency when 5.0 μg NaCN was administered ICV 1 or 5 min prior to MWM testing. No effects were observed when NaCN administration occurred 10 or 15 min prior to testing (Prickaerts et al., 1998).

Conditioned taste aversion. Nachman and Hartley (1975) studied the development of a conditioned taste aversion (CTA) in rats following treatment with CN. Animals were trained to consume their daily water requirement during 10 min of access to a water bottle. On the treatment day, animals were given a 10% sucrose solution instead of water, followed by an intraperitoneal administration of NaCN (2.0 mg/kg). A subsequent decrease in sucrose solution intake, but not water intake, would be indicative of a specific CTA. In this study, no evidence of a CTA was observed, as NaCN-exposed animals consumed equivalent amounts of sucrose solution or water before and after NaCN exposure.

Sensory Responses

Tadic (1992) suggested that CN has antinociceptive effects in rats in a study in which animals were exposed to a low dose of CN (0.6 mg/kg, administered intramuscularly) and tested for sensory reactivity using a hotplate. Compared with saline-treated controls, CN-exposed animals exhibited a significantly longer reaction time on the hotplate test. A rotorod test showed no differences between controls and CN-exposed animals, thereby ruling out a motoric or incapacitating effect at this dose of CN. Interestingly, Tadic also reported that the antinociceptive effects of CN were increased with the addition of the opioid morphine but were decreased with the addition of the opioid antagonist naloxone. Furthermore, two CN antidotes (sodium nitrite and sodium thiosulfate) decreased hotplate reaction time. As a result, Tadic suggested that an endogenous opioid system is involved with CN toxicity.

Neurologic Effects

Using a neurologic index described by Penney, Helfman, Dunbar, and McCoy (1991), Dodds, Penney, and Sutariya (1992) reported deficits in rats 4 hr after a single 4.0 mg/kg intravenous injection of NaCN. The index reflects combined measures (appearance, posture, front-limb walking, circling, activity, and performance on the inverted screen test); it is therefore uncertain whether animals displayed impairment on all or only on certain measures. Others have reported hypoactivity (Kanthasamy et al., 1994) or impaired performance on the inverted screen test (Soine, Brady, Balster, & Underwood, 1980) in KCN or NaCN-exposed rodents, respectively.

Psychological Reactivity

In humans, some individuals suffering from acute panic disorder present with a symptomology showing a degree of similarity with respiratory-distress responses, such as those seen following CN exposure (e.g., respiratory gasp and dizziness; Horwath, Adams, Wickramaratne, Pine, & Weissman, 1997; McNamara, 1976). Similarly, abnormal respiratory physiology has been reported in individuals suffering from panic disorder (Pine et al., 1998). Therefore, it is conceivable that, in a military CN threat arena, a percentage of soldiers who exhibit a predisposition for panic disorder may exhibit symptoms common to both chemical (CN or other) exposure and psychological reactions to suspected or actual exposure.

In an interesting report, a worker in a CN-producing chemical plant who was known to be insensitive to the odor of CN (Nicholson & Vincenti, 1994) gradually developed unusual symptoms while on the job. Initially, when he approached the CN work area, he reported feeling dizzy and weak and developed a headache and shortness of breath. These attacks interfered with job performance as they increased in frequency and severity and eventually began to occur during safety lectures on CN. A severe phobic anxiety for CN was diagnosed, likely associated with combined personal and work-related stress.

Psychological reactivity within a chemical-threat environment is a critical factor in determining situational outcome (see the other articles in this issue). Rapid CN (or other chemical weapon) detection or other means of confirming or dismissing suspicion of CN exposure is therefore required to ensure the application of appropriate medical and logistical procedures.

ANTICYANIDE METHEMOGLOBIN FORMERS AND BEHAVIOR

Among the approaches to counter CN toxicity, certain compounds that form methemoglobin (MHb), including amyl and sodium nitrite ($NaNO_2$), as well as several phenones, such as p-aminophenone (PAPP), p-aminooctanoylphenone (PAOP), and p-aminoheptanoylphenone (PAHP), have shown to be particularly effective (Rockwood et al., 1999). Although effective as anti-CNs, MHb-forming compounds must be used cautiously because MHb formation itself is a form of toxicity compromising oxygen utilization (i.e., hypoxia). Therefore, MHb levels must be carefully monitored to avoid or minimize physiological or behavioral toxic responses.

Experimental Models

Anti-CN effects of $NaNO_2$ in humans have been known for many years (e.g., Chen, Rose, & Clowes, 1935). However, undesirable side effects with $NaNO_2$ have also been noted (Baskin et al., 1992; Weiss, Wilkins, & Haynes, 1937). Kiese and Weger (1969), describing some serious side effects of $NaNO_2$ in humans, reported that the recommended dosage for the treatment of CN poisoning (4.0 mg/kg) resulted in an average of 7% MHb. However, they caution that $NaNO_2$ decreased arterial blood pressure and resulted in orthostatic collapse in several subjects. One subject who received 12.0 mg/kg developed MHb levels reaching approximately 30% and experienced undesirable cardiovascular effects. No additional subjects received this dose.

Although amyl nitrite by inhalation is a rapid method of counteracting cyanide intoxication, it is also an abused drug that gives a giddy high and may increase sexual pleasure. Due to its abuse potential, amyl nitrite is no longer issued to U.S. soldiers.

In humans, several studies evaluated the behavioral effects of the MHb-forming aminophenone PAPP. Paulet, Aubertin, Laurens, and Bourrelier (1963) reported no effects on intellectual functioning, subjective feeling of personal comfort, or physical condition in individuals with up to 48% MHb following oral administration of PAPP. Bodansky and Hendley (1946) reported that MHb levels as high as 30% did not affect visual detection threshold in PAPP-treated subjects, although immediately after exercise, an average of 15% MHb was associated with a significant decrease in visual threshold. Tepperman, Bodansky, and Jandorf (1946) also used PAPP and reported an interaction between exercise load and muscle oxygenation changes. They demonstrated impaired oxygenation of muscle during moderately heavy exercise in subjects with 10% to 20% MHb; however, with light exercise, no effect on muscle oxygenation was observed with 7% to 17% MHb.

Motor function. In rodents, behavioral effects of MHb formers have been studied. For example, Behroozi, Guttman, Gruener, and Shuval (1972) reported decreased locomotor activity following $NaNO_2$; however, MHb levels were not presented. Hlinak and Krejci (1990) also reported decreased locomotor and exploratory activity following treatment with $NaNO_2$. More important, these deficits were long lasting, observed as long as 30 to 50 days after $NaNO_2$ treatment. Freeman, Nielsen, and Gibson (1986) reported dose-dependent locomotor depression in mice treated with 75 to 150 mg/kg $NaNO_2$. In their study, an increase in rest time was accompanied by decreases in total distance traveled, horizontal movements, and vertical movements. In mice, MHb greater than 20% induced by $NaNO_2$, PAPP, or PAHP resulted in a decrease in locomotor activity (Rockwood, Baskin, Romano, & Murrow, 2000).

In an interesting study by Isaacson and Fahey (1987), $NaNO_2$ was shown to impair motor performance on a rotorod, but only when the motor coordination task was preceded by water immersion stress. Isaacson and Fahey suggested that MHb-related hypoxia alone does not directly impair certain motor behaviors, because no differences in MHb levels were observed between stress and nonstressed animals.

Learning. Other investigators studying rodents reported $NaNO_2$-induced performance impairment on a variety of behavioral tasks, including operant tasks (Viveiros & Tondat, 1978) and maze tasks (Reinis, 1970). Hlinak and Krejci (1990) also administered $NaNO_2$ to rats and tested them on the 8-arm radial maze. They observed that working memory was impaired in the $NaNO_2$-treated animals because these animals made significantly more errors than control animals. Gruener (1974) also reported an increase in aggression after treatment with $NaNO_2$, which may be incompatible with optimal learning.

CONCLUSIONS

CN is an inexpensive, readily available synthesized threat agent that can present with rapid, mostly nonpersistent CNS and behavioral effects. Once absorbed, it may also exert delayed CNS actions that are often not associated with the acute CN exposure. Newer technologies must be developed to provide more sensitive CN detection capability, as CN toxicity is, in part, due to CNS effects, although it can affect other excitable tissues as well.

Animal and human studies demonstrate or suggest effects on motor systems, retention of learned avoidance responses, and sensory systems for CN, as well as effects on learning and performance by selective anti-CN countermeasures. When encountered amid the stress and confusion of a CN attack, either on the battlefield or in a civilian catastrophe, CN may present a significant challenge of differential diagnosis to health care personnel.

ACKNOWLEDGMENTS

The opinions or assertions contained herein are the private views of the authors and are not to be construed as official or as reflecting the views of the Army or the Department of Defense. The authors thank library staff members Barbara A. Schultz, Leanna E. Bush, Patricia M. Pepin, Adam S. Szczepaniak, Jr., and Dina C. Puzulis for aid in collecting references for this article.

REFERENCES

Arden, S. R., Sinor, J. D., Potthoff, W. K., & Aizenman, E. (1998). Subunit-specific interactions of cyanide with the N-methyl-D-aspartate receptor. *Journal of Biological Chemistry, 273,* 21505–21511.

Aregheore, E. M., & Agunbiade, O. O. (1991). The toxic effects of cassava (manihot esculenta grantz) diets on humans: A review. *Veterinary and Human Toxicology, 33,* 274–275.

Ashton, D., Van Reempts, J., & Wauquier, A. (1981). Behavioural, electroencephalographic and histological study of the protective effect of etomidate against histotoxic dysoxia produced by cyanide. *Archives Internationales de Pharmacodynamie et de Thérapie, 254,* 196–213.

Ballantyne, B. (1987). Toxicology of cyanides. In B. Ballantyne & T. C. Marrs (Eds.), *Clinical and experimental toxicology of cyanides* (pp. 42–126). Bristol, England: Wright.

Barcroft, J. (1931). The toxicity of atmospheres containing hydrocyanic acid gas. *Journal of Hygiene, 31,* 1–34.

Baskin, S. I., & Brewer, T. G. (1997). Cyanide poisoning. In F. R. Sidell, E. T. Takafuji, & D. R. Franz (Eds.), *Medical aspects of chemical and biological warfare: Textbook of military medicine* (pp. 271–286). Washington, DC: U.S. Department of the Army, Office of the Surgeon General, and Borden Institute.

Baskin, S. I., Horowitz, A. M., & Nealley, E. W. (1992). The antidotal action of sodium nitrite and sodium thiosulfate against cyanide poisoning. *Journal of Clinical Pharmacology, 32,* 368–375.

Behroozi, K., Guttman, R., Gruener, N., & Shuval, H. I. (1972). Changes in the motor activity of mice fed with a sodium nitrite solution. *Israel Journal of Medical Sciences, 8,* 1007.

Blokland, A., Bothmer, J., Honig, W., & Jolles, J. (1993). Behavioural and biochemical effects of acute central metabolic inhibition: Effects of acetyl-l-carnitine. *European Journal of Pharmacology, 235,* 275–281.

Bodansky, O., & Hendley, C. D. (1946). Effect of methemoglobinemia on the visual threshold at sea level. *Journal of Clinical Investigation, 25,* 717–725.

Borowitz, J., Gunasekar, P., & Isom, G. (1997). Hydrogen cyanide generation by mu opiate receptor activation: Possible neuromodulatory role of endogenous cyanide. *Brain Research, 768,* 294–300.

Cai, Z., & McCaslin, P. P. (1992). Selective effects of cyanide (100microM) on the excitatory amino acid-induced elevation of intracellular calcium levels in neuronal culture. *Neurochemistry, 17,* 803–808.

Cassel, G. (1995). Estimation of the convulsive effect of cyanide in cats. *Pharmacology & Toxicology, 77,* 259–263.

Cassel, G., Karlsson, L., & Sellstrom, Å. (1991). On the inhibition of glutamic acid decarboxylase and gamma-aminobutyric acid transaminase by sodium cyanide. *Pharmacology & Toxicology, 69,* 238–241.

Cassel, G., Koch, M., & Tiger, G. (1995). The effects of cyanide on the extracellular levels of dopamine, 3,4-dihydroxyphenylacetic acid, homovanillic acid, 5-hydroxyindoleacetic acid and inositol phospholipid breakdown in the brain. *Neurotoxicology, 16,* 73–82.

Cassel, G., Mjorndal, T., Persson, S.-Å., & Soderstrom, E. (1993). Effects of cyanide on the striatal dopamine receptor binding in the rat. *European Journal of Pharmacology, 248,* 297–301.

Cassel, G., & Persson, S.-Å. (1992). Effects of acute lethal cyanide intoxication on central dopaminergic pathways. *Pharmacology & Toxicology, 70,* 148–151.

Chen, K. K., Rose, C. L., & Clowes, G. H. A. (1935). Cyanide poisoning and its treatment. *Journal of the American Phamaceutical Association, 24,* 625–630.

Coon, J., Glass, H., Sonkin, L. S., & Luahbaugh, C. C. (1943). *Hydrocyanic acid toxicity studies* (University of Chicago Toxicity Laboratory Rep. No. 14, OSRD Rep. No. 1432). Chicago: University of Chicago Toxicity Laboratory.

D'Mello, G. D. (1985). Effects of sodium cyanide upon swimming performance in guinea pigs and the conferment of protection by pretreatment with p-aminopropiophenone. *Neurobehavioral Toxicology and Teratology, 8,* 171–178.

D'Mello, G. D. (1987). Neuropathological and behavioural sequelae of acute cyanide toxicosis in animal species. In B. Ballantyne & T. C. Marrs (Eds.), *Clinical and experimental toxicology of cyanides* (pp. 158–183). Bristol, England: Wright.

Dodds, R. G., Penney, D. G., & Sutariya, B. B. (1992). Cardiovascular, metabolic and neurologic effects of carbon monoxide and cyanide in the rat. *Toxicology Letters, 61,* 243–254.

Evered, M. D., Robinson, M. M., & Rose, P. A. (1988). Effect of arterial pressure on drinking and urinary responses to angiotensin II. *American Journal of Physiology, 254,* R69–R74.

Ferguson, R. L., Ginzler, A. M., Bodansky, O., Boyers, C. L., & Jandorff, B. (1945). *Residual lesions of the central nervous system in cyanide poisoned animals* (Chemical Warfare Service (EA) Medical Division Rep. No. 39). Edgewood Arsenal, MD: Chemical Warfare Service.

Follain, J., & Rufford, N. (2001, October 14). Cyanide threat: Tapes reveal poison plan. *The Sunday Times.* Retrieved October 22, 2001, from http:www.sunday-times.co.uk/news/pages/sti/2001/10/14/stiusausa01025.html

Fowler, R. C., & Durbetaki, A. J. (1952). Cyanide and thiocyanate determination in multiple sclerosis and allied demyelinizing disorders. *American Journal of Physiology, 171,* 724.

Freeman, G. B., Nielsen, P., & Gibson, G. E. (1986). Monoamine neurotransmitter metabolism and locomotor activity during chemical hypoxia. *Journal of Neurochemistry, 46,* 733–738.

Garbuz, A. M. (1971). Functional state of the central nervous system in symptomless methemoglobinemia. *Gigiena Sanitorium, 36,* 101–103. (UDC–NTIS No. 124–126)

Grey, S., & Gadher, D. (2001, October 7). Terror camps: Inside Bin Laden's academies of terror. *The Sunday Times.* Retrieved October 22, 2001, from http:www.sunday-times.co.uk/news/pages/sti/2001/10/07/stiusausa02016.html

Gruener. N. (1974). The effects of nitrites on isolation-induced aggression in mice. *Pharmacology, Biochemistry and Behavior, 2,* 267–269.

Haymaker, W., Ginzler, A. M., & Ferguson, R. L. (1952). Residual neuropathological effects of cyanide poisoning: A study of the central nervous system of 23 dogs exposed to cyanide compounds. *The Military Surgeon, 3,* 231–246.

Heylin, M. (1988). U.S. decries apparent chemical arms attack. *Chemical Engineering News, 6,* 23.

Hlinak, Z., & Krejci, I. (1990). Long-term behavioural consequences of sodium nitrite hypoxia: An animal model. *Activitas Nervosa Supererior, 32,* 48–49.

Holland, M. A., & Kozlowski, L. M. (1986). Clinical features and management of cyanide poisoning. *Clinical Pharmacology, 5,* 737–741.

Horwath, E., Adams, P., Wickramaratne, P., Pine, D., & Weissman, M. M. (1997). Panic disorder with smothering symptoms: Evidence for increased risk in first-degree relatives. *Depression and Anxiety, 6,* 147–153.

Howlett, W. P., Brubaker, G. R., Mlingi, N., & Rosling, H. (1990). Konzo, an epidemic upper motor neuron disease studied in Tanzania. *Brain, 113,* 223–235.

Hurst, E. W. (1940). Experimental demyelination of the central nervous system: 1. The encephalopathy produced by potassium cyanide. *Australian Journal of Experimental Biological Medical Science, 18,* 201–223.

Isaacson, R. L., & Fahey, J. M. (1987). Some anatomical and behavioral consequences of acute sodium nitrite administration. *Neuroscience Research Communications, 1,* 39–45.

Johnson, R. P., & Mellors, J. W. (1988). Arteriolization of venous blood gases: A clue to the diagnosis of cyanide poisoning. *Journal of Emergency Medicine, 6,* 401–404.

Kanthasamy, A. G., Borowitz, J. L., Pavlakovic, G., & Isom, G. E. (1994). Dopaminergic neurotoxicity of cyanide: Neurochemical, histological, and behavioral characterization. *Toxicology and Applied Pharmacology, 126,* 156–163.

Keilin, D. (1929). Cytochrome and respiratory enzymes. *Proceedings of the Royal Society B, 104,* 206–252.

Kiese, M., & Weger, N. (1969). Formation of ferrihaemoglobin with aminophenols in the human for the treatment of cyanide poisoning. *European Journal of Pharmacology, 7,* 97–105.

Lang, J. S., Mullin, D., Fenyvesi, C., Rosenberg, R., & Barnes, J. (1986, November 10). Is the protector of lions losing his touch? *U.S. News & World Report,* p. 29.

Langston, J. W., Ballard, P., Terrud, J. W., & Irwin, I. (1983). Chronic Parkinsonism in humans due to product of meperidine-analog synthesis. *Science, 219,* 979–980.

Levin, B. C., Paabo, M., Gurman, J. L., Clark, H. M., & Yoklavich, M. F. (1988). Further studies of the toxicological effects of different time exposures to the individual and combined fire gases—Carbon monoxide, hydrogen cyanide, carbon dioxide and reduced oxygen. In *Polyurethanes '88: Proceedings of the Society of the Plastics Industry, 31st Annual Technical/Marketing Conference* (pp. 249–252). Washington, DC.

Lipton, B. S. (1947). Blocking of chemical decerebration by pontile pathology. *Journal of Nervous and Mental Diseases, 106,* 537–539.

Lundquist, P., Rosling, H., & Sorbo, B. (1988). The origin of hydrogen cyanide in breath. *Archives of Toxicology, 61,* 270–274.

Macy, R. (1937). *Hydrocyanic acid: Its military history and a summary of its properties* (Edgewood Arsenal Tech. Rep. No. 219). Edgewood Arsenal, MD: War Department, Chemical Warfare Service. (DTIC No. AD–B957 032)

Mangun, G. H., & Skipper, H. E. (1942). *Hydrocyanic acid: The toxicity and speed of action on man* (Edgewood Arsenal Memorandum Rep. Project A 3.5–1, Technical Directorate Memorandum Rep. No. 471). Aberdeen Proving Ground, MD: Chemical Warfare Service.

Marrs, T. C., Bright, J. E., & Swanson, D. W. (1982). Acute oral toxicity of 4-dimethylaminophenol to the gastrointestinal tract, liver and kidney of the rat. *Archives of Toxicology, 50,* 89–92.

McCaslin, P. P., & Yu, Z. Z. (1992). Cyanide selectively augments kainate- but not NMDA-induced release of glutamate and taurine. *European Journal of Pharmacology, 228,* 73–75.

McMahon, T. F., & Birnbaum, L. S. (1990). Age-related changes in toxicity and biotransformation of potassium cyanide in male C57BL/6N mice. *Toxicology and Applied Pharmacology, 105,* 305–314.

McNamara, B. P. (1976). *Estimates of the toxicity of hydrocyanic acid vapors in man* (Edgewood Arsenal Tech. Rep. No. EB–TR–76023). Aberdeen Proving Ground, MD: U.S. Biomedical Laboratory. (DTIC No. AD–2101)

Medical expert reports use of chemical weapons in Iran–Iraq war. (1985). *U.N. Chronicle, 22,* 24–26.

Messing, B., & Storch, B. (1988). Computer tomography and magnetic resonance imaging in cyanide poisoning. *European Archives of Psychiatry and Neurological Sciences, 237,* 139–143.

Mills, E. M., Gunasekar, P. G., Li, L., Borowitz, J. L., & Isom, G. E. (1999). Differential susceptibility of brain areas to cyanide involves different modes of cell death. *Toxicology and Applied Pharmacology, 156,* 6–16.

Nachman, N., & Hartley, P. L. (1975). Role of illness in producing learned taste aversion in rats: A comparison of several rodenticides. *Journal of Comparative and Physiological Psychology, 89,* 1010–1018.

Nicholson, P. J., & Vincenti, G. E. P. (1994). A case of phobic anxiety related to the inability to smell cyanide. *Occupational Medicine (London), 44,* 107–108.

Oehler, G. C. (1996, March 27). *The growing chemical and biological weapons threat* (Testimony before the Permanent Subcommittee on Investigations of the Senate Committee on Government Affairs). Retrieved October 22, 2001, from http://www.kimsoft.com/korea/ciachem1.htm

Orii, Y. (1985). Exclusive CO binding to cytochrome oxidase. *Journal of Inorganic Biochemistry, 23,* 263–271.

Patel, M. N., Peoples, R. W., Yim, G. K., & Isom, G. E. (1994). Enhancement of NMDA-mediated responses by cyanide. *Neurochemical Research, 19,* 1319–1323.

Patel, M. N., Yim, G. K., & Isom, G. E. (1992). Potentiation of cyanide neurotoxicity by blockade of ATP-sensitive potassium channels. *Brain Research, 593,* 114–116.

Patel, M. N., Yim, G. K., & Isom, G. E. (1993). N-methyl-D-aspartate receptors mediate cyanide-induced cytotoxicity in hippocampal cultures. *Neurotoxicology, 14,* 35–40.

Paulet, G. (1955) De l'importance relative de la défaillance respiratoire et de la défaillance cardiaque dans l'action lethale des cyanures [The relative importance of respiratory failure and cardiac failure in the fatal action of cyanide]. *Archives de Internationales Physiologie et de Biochimie, 63,* 328–339.

Paulet, G., Aubertin, X., Laurens, L., & Bourrelier, J. (1963). De l'action methemoglobinisante de la paraaminopropiophenone chez l'homme—Avec un complement experimental chez le chien [On the methemoglobinizing effect of paraaminopropiophenone in man—With an experimental complement in the dog]. *Archives Internationales de Pharmacodynamie et de Therapie, 142,* 35–51.

Penney, D. G., Helfman, C. C., Dunbar, J. C., & McCoy, L. E. (1991). Acute severe carbon monoxide exposure in the rat: Effects of hyperglycemia and hypoglycemia on mortality, recovery, and neurological deficit. *Canadian Journal of Physiology, 69,* 1168–1177.

Persson, S.-Å., Cassel, G., & Sellström, Å. (1985). Acute cyanide intoxication and central transmitter systems. *Fundamental and Applied Toxicology, 5,* S150–S159.

Piantadosi, C. A., & Sylvia, A. L. (1984). Cerebral cytochrome a,a_3 inhibition by cyanide in bloodless rats. *Toxicology, 33,* 67–79.

Pine, D. S., Coplan, J. D., Papp, L. A., Klein, R. G., Martinez, J. M., Kovalenko, P., et al. (1998). Ventilatory physiology of children and adolescents with anxiety disorder. *Archives of General Psychiatry, 55,* 123–129.

Prickaerts, J., Blokland, A., Bothmer, J., Honig, W., Markerink-Van Ittersum, M., & Jolles, J. (1998). Acute effects of acetyl-L-carnitine on sodium cyanide-induced behavioral and biochemical deficits. *Neurochemistry International, 33,* 435–443.

Radonjic, V., Boskovic, B., & Pribic, A. (1983). Hitna pomoc kod trovanja cijanovodonikom prilikom fumigacije [Emergency treatment in case of cyanide poisoning during fumigation]. *Arhiv Za Higijenu Rada I Toksikologiju, 34,* 238–249.

Reinis, S. (1970). Effect of hydroxylamine on maze learning in mice. *Journal of Comparative and Physiological Psychology, 72,* 512–518.

Rockwood, G. A., Baskin, S. I., Romano, J. A., Jr., & Murrow, M. L. (2000). *Effects of methemoglobin formers on spontaneous locomotor activity and methemoglobin levels in mice* (Tech. Rep. No. USAMRICD-TR-00-06). Aberdeen Proving Ground, MD: U.S. Army Medical Research Institute of Chemical Defense.

Rockwood, G. A., Baskin, S. I., Romano, J. A., Jr., Murrow, M. L., Preville, J. A., Lee, R. B., et al. (1999). Comparison of hematologic consequences and efficacy of p-aminophenones in mice. *Environmental Toxicology and Pharmacology, 7,* 237–252.

Rose, C. L., Harris, P. N., & Chen, K. K. (1954). Effect of cyanide poisoning on the central nervous system of rats and dogs. *Proceedings of the Society of Experimental Biology & Medicine, 87,* 632–636.

Rosenow, F., Herholz, K., Lanfermann, H., Weuthen, R., & Heiss, W.-D. (1995). Neurological sequelae of cyanide intoxication—The patterns of clinical, magnetic resonance imaging, and positron emission tomography findings. *Annals of Neurology, 38,* 825–829.

Soine, W. H., Brady, K. T., Balster, R. L., & Underwood, J. Q., III. (1980). Chemical and behavioral studies of l-piperidinocyclohexanecarbonitrile (PCC): Evidence for cyanide as the toxic component. *Research Communications in Chemical Pathology and Pharmacology, 30,* 59–70.

Sollmann, T. (1948). *A manual of pharmacology and its applications to therapeutics and toxicology* (7th ed.). Philadelphia: Saunders.

Sun, P., Rane, S. G., Gunasekar, P. G., Borowitz, J. L., & Isom, G. E. (1999). Cyanide interaction with redox modulatory sites enhances NMDA receptor responses. *Journal of Biochemical & Molecular Toxicology, 13,* 253–259.

Tadic. V. (1992). The possible role of the system of endogenous opioids in the mechanism of cyanide toxicity. *Acta Veterinaria (Beograd), 42,* 43–52.

Tepperman, J., Bodansky, O., & Jandorf, B. (1946). The effect of para-aminophenone-induced methemoglobinemia on oxygenation of working muscle in human subjects. *American Journal of Physiology, 146,* 702–709.

Trapp, W. G. (1970). Massive cyanide poisoning with recovery: A Boxing-day story. *Canadian Medical Association Journal, 102,* 517.

Tylleskär, T., Banea, M., Bikangi, N., Fresco, L., Persson, L.-Å., & Rosling, H. (1991). Epidemiological evidence from Zaire for a dietary etiology of konzo, an upper motor neuron disease. *Bulletin of the World Health Organization, 69,* 581–589.

Tylleskär, T., Banea, M., Bikangi, N., Nahimana, G., Persson, L.-Å., & Rosling, H. (1995). Dietary determinants of a non-progressive spastic paraparesis (konzo): A case-referent study in a high incidence area of Zaire. *International Journal of Epidemiology, 24,* 949–956.

Uitti, R. J., Rajput, A. H., Ashenhurst, E. M., & Rozdilsky, B. (1985). Cyanide-induced Parkinsonism: A clinicopathologic report. *Neurology, 35,* 921–925.

Van Buuren, K. J. H., Nicholls, P., & Van Gelder, B. F. (1972). Biochemical and biophysical studies on cytochrome aa3: VI. Reaction of cyanide with oxidized and reduced enzyme. *Biochimica Biophysica Acta, 256,* 258–276.

Vincent, F. M. (1986). Pathologic changes after cyanide poisoning. *Neurology, 36,* 137.

Vincent, M., Vincent, F., Marka, C., & Faure, J. (1981). Cyanide and its relationship to nervous suffering: Physiopathological aspects of intoxication. *Clinical Toxicology, 18,* 1519–1527.

Viveiros, D. M., & Tondat, L. (1978). Effects of sodium nitrite on DRL performance in the rat. *Pharmacology, Biochemistry and Behavior, 8,* 125–127.

Vogel, S. N., Sultan, T. R., & Ten Eyck, R. P. (1981). Cyanide poisoning. *Clinical Toxicology, 18,* 367–383.

Warburg, O. (1925). Über Eisen, den sauerstoffübertragenden Bestandteil des Atmungsferments [On iron, the oxygen-transferring constituent of the respiratory system]. *Berichte der Deutschen Chemischen Gesellschaft, 58,* 1001–1011.

Warburg, O., Negelein, E., & Haas, E. (1933). Spektroskopischer Nachweis des sauerstoffübertradenden Ferments neben Cytochrom [Spectroscopic evidence of the oxygen-transferring ferment compared to cytochrome]. *Biochemische Zeitschrift, 266,* 1–8.

Way, J. L. (1981). Pharmacological aspects of cyanide and antagonism. In B. Vennesland, E. E. Conn, J. Knowles, & J. Westley (Eds.), *Cyanide in biology* (pp. 29–49). London: Academic.

Way, J. L. (1984). Cyanide intoxication and its mechanism of antagonism. *Annual Review of Pharmacology and Toxicology, 24,* 451–481.

Way, J. L., Sylvester, D., Morgan, R. L., Isom, G. E., Burrows, G. E., Tamulinas, C. B., et al. (1984). Recent perspectives on the toxicodynamic basis of cyanide antagonism. *Fundamental and Applied Toxicology, 4,* S231–S239.

Weger, N. (1969). *Treatment of hydrocyanic acid poisoning by the formation of methemoglobin.* Unpublished doctoral dissertation, Pharmacological Institute of the University of Munich, Germany.

Weiss, S., Wilkins, R. W., & Haynes, F. W. (1937). The nature of circulatory collapse induced by sodium nitrite. *The Journal of Clinical Investigation, 16,* 73–84.

Williams, P., & Wallace, D. (1989). *Unit 731: Japan's secret biological warfare in World War II.* New York: Free Press.

Made in the USA
Las Vegas, NV
29 October 2024

10614935R10056